MW00682845

COMPUTERS

MADE

Really EASY

FOR BEGINNERS

by

Norma Leonardi Leone

LION PRESS & VIDEO

Rochester, New York

Computers Made *Really* Easy for Beginners

Copyright © 1995 by Lion Press & Video

All rights reserved. No part of this book may be reproduced or transmitted in any form or by any means, electronic or mechanical, including photocopying, recording, or by any information storage and retrieval system, without the permission in writing from the publisher, with the exception of brief quotations for review.

Inquires should be addressed to:

Lion Press & Video
P.O. Box 92541
Rochester, NY 14692

Cover and graphics design by Antoinette Follett
Typesetting and Electronic Editing by Tony Leone

Printed in the United States of America

Library of Congress Cataloging-in-Publication Data

Leone, Norma Leonardi, 1935-
        Computers made really easy for beginners / by Norma Leonardi Leone.
                p.   cm.
        Includes index.
        ISBN 0-936635-08-8 (pbk.)
        1. Microcomputers.   I. Title.
QA76.5.L464 1995
004. 165--dc20

                                                                95-294
                                                                CIF

For Tony

Who made this book possible

With his help, his inspiration
and his love

PREFACE

If you recognize the need to learn about computers but think of Pascal as a type of celery and software as a material for warm, cozy nightgowns, this book is for you.

Even if you haven't learned any math or science since your early high school years (and that was longer ago than you care to admit), don't presume that learning to use a computer would be about as easy for you as learning quantum physics.

Although your primary concerns in recent years may have been related to your job or family, you still can (and should) learn to use a computer. Contrary to what many people think, a computer is not a foreboding, mysterious technological device that only a junior Einstein can master. A computer is a practical, efficient instrument that can save you time and energy—a work-saver that *anyone* can learn to use.

I know. I was one of the many women who spent the greater part of her adult life being a wife and mother, homemaker, and volunteer everything. Those were worthwhile and rewarding activities, but they did little to help me understand anything like a computer. What is worse, I had successfully avoided anything involving mathematics or science since high school ("Girls don't need to know those things" was the advice in those days, and I believed it). I still avoid dealing with anything technical or mathematical, but I did learn to use a computer. You can, too. Learning to use a computer, like so many other skills, is largely a matter of developing confidence (in your abilities) and understanding (of the computer's capabilities). Once you have that confidence and understanding, you will discover that a computer can help you, teach you, and even entertain you—among other things. The possibilities are endless.

Learning to use a computer does take time and effort. But if you put forth that time and effort, you'll have access to a fascinating, challenging device that can help you thrive during the information age that is well under way.

Table of Contents

CHAPTER 1

UNDERSTANDING THE COMPUTER AND WHAT IT CAN DO FOR YOU

You Are in Charge Around Here

A computer is an electronic device that stores instructions and information and also calculates, compiles, correlates and selects all this information—at your command—very, very fast. A computer is most notable because of the huge amounts of information it can store and the speed and accuracy with which it uses that information. Because of all this speed, accuracy and storage capacity, popular myths about the computer abound.

Understanding the computer involves dispelling some of those myths about what a computer can and cannot do. For example, a computer cannot organize your life or your files, your records, your finances, your business or anything else *unless* you (or someone else) gathers all the necessary information and puts it into the computer in a format the computer recognizes. The format used to put the information into the computer is decided by something called a *program*.

A program, also known as *software,* can be written to organize just about anything you want, but the computer doesn't do any of this organizing by itself. A computer has no brain; it cannot think, reason, or make decisions on its own, and it definitely is not smarter than you. Faster, yes. Smarter, no.

All computers must have a program to provide highly detailed instructions for exactly what to do, when to do it, and how to do it. Without such a program, a computer is practically useless. Thousands of programs are available to perform just about any type of task, but until you have a program installed on your computer (or loaded from disks), a computer will do little more than flash a character or message on the screen.

A computer more than makes up for what it can't do, however, with its ability to perform many incredible tasks with equally incredible speed and accuracy--but only after it has a set of instructions from a program and information from you. The key here is *you.* The more you understand about the computer and the programs you use, the more you can make it do for you.

Computer programs are available to do just about any task you need done, and when you use a computer to perform a task, the computer program you use is called an *application.* Computer programs (which are called *software*) are

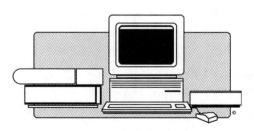

explained in Chapter 3 of this book. But for now, let's just look at some of the many tasks computer *application programs (or software)* can do for you:

COMPUTER APPLICATION PROGRAMS:

WORD PROCESSING

The most common use for personal computers is for word processing. A word processing program allows you to use your computer somewhat like an electronic typewriter, but one that does much more than any ordinary typewriter. By using a word processing program, information can be entered from a keyboard (or copied from a disk) and displayed on a screen so that you can insert, delete, or rearrange the sequence of letters, words, lines, or whole paragraphs before they are printed on paper. You can also arrange these words, lines and paragraphs in any number of ways, such as centered on the page, in columns, with justified (aligned) margins, or in any combination of these formats—all at the touch of a few keys.

A word processing program makes even a self-correcting typewriter seem obsolete, since corrections can be made before anything is printed. Many word processing programs also have other types of assistance available, such as a spelling checker that will search through the document to find misspelled words and a grammar checker that will look for grammatical and writing mistakes and a thesaurus to allow you to look up alternative words to enhance your writing.

When using a word processing program, once the document, letter, or whatever you are creating is completed to your satisfaction, you can have the computer print it out or have it stored for recall whenever you want, and then used, changed, and/or stored again and again.

Word processing programs have expanded to do all types of tasks that at one time could be done only on very expensive equipment. Many word processing programs now have the ability to use a wide selection of typefaces, graphics, and characters so that you can create newsletters, invitations, announcements, greeting cards, programs, brochures and the like with your computer.

Word processing can be carried one step further if you have a modem: you can then use your telephone line to connect your computer to compatible equipment, such as a typesetter, so that it is possible to put together a newsletter or report and have it typeset directly from your computer.

STORE, ORGANIZE, SORT, AND SELECT INFORMATION

You can use a computer program to store any type of documents, such as inventories, records, files, financial data, reports, accounts, or any of type of information.

Once this information is in the computer, you can use a program to organize the information in any number of different ways. For example, a computer program can store a list of names and addresses for a business, club, organization, department, group or whatever, and then file and recall the list alphabetically by name, company, location, Zip Code, business or membership type. A program can also recall the information in any combination of ways, such as all the people in one area and who run one type of business and who have spent more than a certain amount in the last six months. Any of this information can be changed easily at the touch of a key.

You can use a computer program to store financial information and then do comparisons, projections, or analyses of the information and show the results in figures or percentages, in graphs or charts, or in any combination of these formats.

Computer programs are available that will keep records of investments, insurance policies, stocks and bonds and bank accounts, and then show the financial returns on each of them, compare the rate of return with each other, or compare the rate of return with other investments you may be considering.

CALCULATE FIGURES

You can use a computer program to print out checks, balance your checkbook, and figure and print out your taxes. Computer programs can also be used to separate, itemize, and calculate business, entertainment, household, medical and other expenses, compare them to budgeted amounts, show the amounts as percentage of income or deductible expenses, or list them in a number of other formats. You can use a computer program to calculate mortgage and loan payments at different rates and repayment plans, to compare interest compounded at varying rates, to figure depreciation on cars, boats, or any other belongings, to do metric conversions and to change, update, and recalculate any of this information at any time--and to do all of this very fast.

A calculator will also perform all the functions mentioned above, but a computer can handle large groups of numbers, perform multiple calculations with them, and store all the numbers and the results of the calculations for recall later.

ACCESS INFORMATION SERVICES

If you have a device called a *modem* with your computer, the modem can convert your computer signals into a form that can be sent or received over your telephone line. You can then use the modem to find a wealth of information on subjects ranging from antiques to zero gravity.

A modem can connect your computer to other larger computers which contain information organized in *databases*. Databases are collections of related information that have been categorized, generally by subject, and then stored in a computer file. Because databases are available

by using telephone lines, they are often called online databases, and using this kind of database is sometimes called going "online."

You can obtain information from databases by subscribing directly to the database or by subscribing to an online information service or other information

utility that gives you access to a number of other databases. Although the terms database, online information services, and information services or utilities are often used interchangeably, they are not exactly alike. Individual databases usually contain one type of information (such as financial, legal or scientific), and the online information services (or utilities) are collections of information gathered from several databases.

You can subscribe to either or both types of these services, although subscribing to individual databases is more expensive than subscribing to an information service. By subscribing to databases or information services, you can use your computer to gain access to information that has been gathered from national and international wire services, newspapers, books, magazines, and many other sources previously available only from a library or the source of the original information. In addition, most databases are available 24 hours a day, 7 days a week, so you can access this information any time you want.

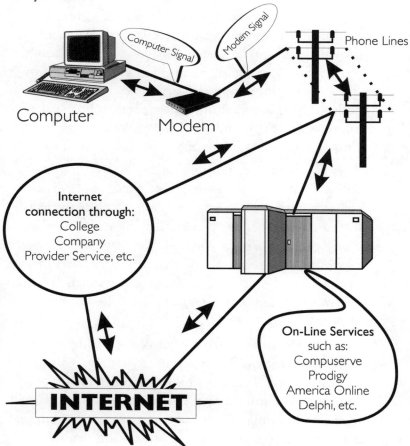

Computer Online Connections

Although commercial databases and online services generally charge some type of fee for their services, much information is also available at no charge by using your modem to connect to *bulletin boards.* A bulletin board is often run by local or area computer user groups, and many of them provide a wide range of information on a variety of subjects--all at no charge.

A few of the many types of databases include those that provide news and weather reports, stock quotations, gardening information, financial and real estate listings, travel information, energy and environmental updates, agricultural information and farm news, medical and health-related information, college test and financial aid information, movie and television reviews, government reports, soap opera summaries, and much, much more.

The amount of information available from these online databases is staggering. One database offers the complete text of the *New York Times* as well as abstracts from a dozen other newspapers, including *The Washington Post, Los Angeles Times, The Wall Street Journal,* and *The Christian Science Monitor.* Another database offers indexes to stories from more than 1,100 magazines such as *Time, Newsweek, Better Homes and Gardens, Life,* and *Bon Appetit.*

The information from databases is filed by subject name and category. When you use a database, you provide a word or category to indicate the specific or general type of information you need. The computer will then search through all the information contained in that database and show you what is available on that subject. You can then scan through the information displayed and select any (or all) of the information you want to see. The information could range from a newspaper editorial to a complete listing of everything on that subject from an encyclopedia, or it could be the full text of an article from a magazine or journal, an abstract of an article, a reference to an article or story, or a combination of all of these resources.

If you have a printer with your computer, all this information can be printed out and then used at your leisure. Some databases make it possible to use your computer to order copies of whole stories and articles for which the database provides a reference (there may be an extra charge for this service, but the charge is often no more than $1.00 to $3.00, which may be less than the cost of driving to your local library). Subscribing to a database is like having a librarian available for any amount of research on any type of information you need at any time you want!

SEND AND RECEIVE MESSAGES

You can also use your modem to exchange information by accessing computer bulletin boards and electronic mail boxes. Bulletin boards provide a way for computer users to place messages for other computer users to read (and respond to if they want), and electronic mailboxes provide a way to use your computer to send and receive messages from other computer users. Placing a message on a computer bulletin board is similar to posting a message on any bulletin board; that is, anyone can read it. Sending and receiving a message via an electronic mailbox is similar to sending a message in the mail; that is, the message is sent to one person or company at one address.

Bulletin boards and mail boxes, whose functions are very similar, allow computer users to "talk" to each other, exchange information on a wide variety of personal and business interests (often not having anything to do with the computer), meet new people with similar interests, and sometimes share computer programs, all by going online from their own computers.

If you've been hearing about the Internet and the "Information Superhighway," this is it. Electronic mail, or E-mail is cheaper, faster, and more efficient than any other method of exchanging information. Your computer can be an information and communication source that can't be matched anywhere else.

PRINT TEXT, GRAPHICS, CHARTS, GRAPHS AND MORE

By using a printer connected to your computer, you can print out a copy of any document created on your computer (the printed copy is called a "hard copy "). Hundreds of different types of printers are available today and can produce copies in a wide range of sizes and qualities. Printers that are readily available today allow you to print with proportional spacing, use a wide variety of fonts, print with typeset quality, and print in color.

Some types of printers can also reproduce drawings, diagrams, charts and other graphics, providing valuable assistance for certain types of work. Color printers are especially nice for printing charts, graphs, and for graphic images, but they can also add appeal to almost any type of printed information.

A printer not only can print out the letters and other documents, but can also print out mailing labels, envelopes, letters, forms, checks, bills, overhead transparencies and more. In addition, papers that can be used in a printer now come in a wide variety of types, styles, colors, and weights. You can now produce some very professional looking documents that were once available only from better typesetting services.

PROVIDE EDUCATIONAL AND INSTRUCTIONAL CAPABILITIES

Computer programs are available to provide instructions in just about any type of learning. You can use a computer program to learn foreign languages, mathematics, science, history, diet planning, budgeting, health care, and much more. You can even use a learning program to show you how to take advantage of some of the more complex features of both computers and programs.

Instructional computer pro-grams can help you with your own learning and are generally designed to allow you to work and learn at your own pace. These programs can make it easier for you to help your children with their computer homework—or make it easier for them to help you!

Special educational programs are also available for people who have learning disabilities or handicaps, and these programs can be an invaluable aid in providing both instruction and communication capabilities. In addition, several databases offer informa-tion prepared especially for handicapped individuals.

PLAY COMPUTER GAMES

Computer games are popular with many personal computer users. A wide variety of games is available to available to suit any taste, age group, or interest level. Some computer games are challenging or educational, but most are just plain fun. Many of the newer game programs come complete with sound, graphics, animation and much more.

CREATE SPECIAL TYPES OF DOCUMENTS

Programs are available for creating all types of special documents, such as graphics (drawings, figures, illustrations) and animation. Engineering options such as CAD (computer-aided design or CAM (computer-aided manufacturing) are used for engineering types of tasks. Specialized publishing programs are available for use in creating books and magazines. Although many word processing programs contain desktop publishing capabilities, including special features for designing pages of text for books and pamphlets, there are also special desktop publishing programs available specifically for this and other printing and publishing purposes.

PERFORM SPECIAL TASKS

Highly special programs that combine many of the features above are available for just about any type of business or profession, such as financial, medical, legal, accounting, educational, fund-raising, and many others. Order entry and tracking, inventory control, patient records, legal records, and library card catalogs, are a few of the many types of tasks that can be handled quickly and efficiently with a computer program. Mail order business are now putting their entire catalogs on computer disks or on a CD-ROM (Compact Disk-Read Only Memory) so that you can browse through the catalog and place an order from your computer. Encycylopaedias, manuals, atlases, and dictionaries are available on CD-ROM or computer disk now, and more and more business and services are offering their products on computer disk or CD-ROM.

SEND AND RECEIVE DOCUMENTS

The ability to send and receive documents directly from your computer is a feature that is built in to many of the programs available today. This feature is like using a *facsimile (or fax,* as it is commonly called) machine, but the document is sent directly from your computer. You need to have a fax modem board installed in your computer to use this feature, but once the fax capabilities are set up, you no longer have to print out documents and put them into a fax machine to send them. You can send and receive faxes directly from your computer without ever having to print them out.

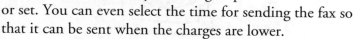

Some programs allow you to store names and phone numbers so that you don't have to enter this information each time you send a fax. You can also store this information so that it is saved in groups or sets of people or companies and then have the computer fax the same document to everyone in a group or set. You can even select the time for sending the fax so that it can be sent when the charges are lower.

The programs and uses for a computer described in this chapter are a few of the major types of programs, but there are many, many more. You do not necessarily have to buy a program for each task you want to do. Many programs are specifically designed to do one task, but more and more programs today include the ability to perform many tasks. Some of these programs are called *integrated* programs and offer a combination of programs such as a spreadsheet, database and word processing program. The commands are usually interchangeable between each program and make learning easier and faster.

In addition, many programs designed to do one task now offer additional capabilities within that program. For example, several word processing programs now include database, spreadsheet, graphics, charting, desktop publishing and faxing capabilities.

So, if you have any type of work to be done, a hobby or interest to explore, games you want to play, or information you need to look up or exchange, a computer program is available to help you. You may find one program that will fill all your needs, or you may want to have separate programs for each task. But no matter what your needs or goals, a computer program is available to make your work (or play) easier, faster, and better.

CHAPTER 2

THE PARTS OF A COMPUTER AND HOW THEY WORK
The Fastest Helper You'll Ever Find

Before you put the computer to work for you, it is helpful to understand something about the various components that make up a computer and what they do. It is possible to use a computer without ever learning very much about its components, but you'll understand computers better if you have a little background knowledge about the parts of a computer and their effect on what the computer can do.

Computers come in hundreds of styles and sizes, from the huge mainframes that can fill an entire room to the newest pocket-sized portable variety. The physical size of the computer does not necessarily reflect the amount of work the computer can do or the speed with which it can do that work. Actually, newer computers are frequently smaller than older ones and can do more tasks and do them considerably faster. But no matter what the size or style, most computers share the following common parts:

HARDWARE AND SOFTWARE

The physical parts that make up the computer are called *hardware*. The computer itself, the monitor, keyboard, and accessories such as a printer (called *peripherals or components*) are all hardware.

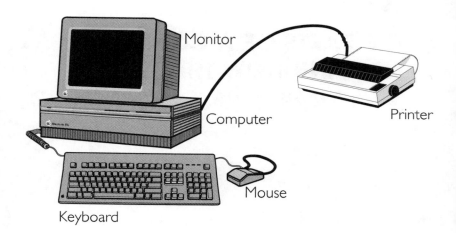

Monitor

Computer

Printer

Mouse

Keyboard

Parts of a Computer System

Programs are called *software*. Programs provide instructions to run the computer and to perform special types of tasks, as described in the previous chapter. But all programs are called software, and the names programs and software are used interchangeably.

OPERATING SYSTEM

All computers *must* have an operating system to work. The operating system is a very special program that tells the computer about the keyboard, disk drives, monitor, and so forth, so it can later carry out the instructions of the various programs the computer uses. The operating system is inside the computer and a part that you don't see and many don't think about. But it is inside *every* computer. Most personal IBM-compatible computers use MS-DOS (Microsoft Disk operating system), although other operating systems, such as OS/2, DR-DOS, Novell 7, IBM-DOS, and so forth, are also used. Apple and Macintosh computer have their own operating systems.

"Windows" is a program that makes it easier to use MS-DOS by substituting pictures (or symbols, called *icons*) for words. The concept of using pictures for words is called GUI, for Graphical user interface. "Interface" describes how you access information in your computer, so a Graphical user interface allows you to select icons to load programs, move files, and so forth, rather than entering text to do these tasks.

Scientific, business and special computers may use other types of operating systems such as Unix, VMS, or others that perform the same functions as MS-DOS but that are specialized for certain kinds of operations.

Many computers, especially those used in business operations, are set up on a computer "Network." This means the computers are all linked together in a way that allows them to share data and programs.

KEYBOARD

A keyboard is commonly used for entering instructions and information into the computer (although, in some instances, this can also be done by a magnetic tape or disk, by one of the new voice recognition programs or by a pen-based computer).

The keyboard is similar to a standard typewriter keyboard in appearance, but a computer keyboard has more keys. The additional keys usually are labeled with names such as *Enter, Home, Control, Escape,* or with symbols such as arrows or other characters. If you're using an IBM-compatible computer, there is an extra row of keys at the top or side of the keyboard; these keys are usually labeled F1, F2, F3 (or SF1, SF2), and so on, and are called *function* keys. These extra keys allow the computer to do much more than any typewriter.

The extra keys on the computer keyboard are usually used for instructions and commands or to move easily and quickly around the screen. The keys on the computer keyboard respond differently from a typewriter key in both touch and action. When you press a typewriter key, even on an electric typewriter, you must press down because you need to activate some mechanical element. Pressing a key also produces some kind of response: a letter appears on the paper, or the carriage moves, or something happens.

When you press a key on a computer keyboard, however, you only need to activate an electrical signal, so the touch action is considerably lighter. Also, when you press a key on a computer keyboard, it is quite possible that nothing apparent will happen; it is also quite possible that a whole program will run. What happens after you press a key on a computer keyboard depends on what instructions or programs the computer is carrying out at the time.

Because of the typewriter-like keyboard, it is helpful to be able to type, but certainly not essential. Many people who have advanced degrees in computer science or engineering have no formal keyboard entry training and thus use the two-finger method to enter complex computer programs or data that may contain thousands of entries.

MONITOR (OR "SCREEN")

A computer monitor is used to show you what the computer is doing. The monitor doesn't show *everything* the computer is doing, but it does show you what you are entering, where you are in a program, or whatever you have directed it to tell you. Most monitors look like a television screen, and some older computers do use an actual television set as a monitor (these monitors can be switched at any time to regular television programming).

Most computers today have a special screen that can be used only for computer display. The information displayed on the monitor appears only during the actual operation of the computer and disappears when the computer is turned off.

A computer monitor can display characters or images, in monochrome (using one color, often yellow, green or white), or it can display characters and images in full color. Color monitors are, of course, more expensive than the monochrome ones. But like all computer components these days, color monitors are becoming more common and more reasonably priced as time goes on.

The quality of the display also depends on the type of monitor you are using. Many newer monitors have color displays of a very high quality that produce extremely sharp images in brilliant colors.

At one time, most computer monitors were relatively small (usually 9" measured diagonally, and some were smaller), but monitors are now available in much larger sizes, such as 15" or 17" or 20" or larger. These larger monitors make is easy to read side-by-side pages and to view graphics and color with much more clarity. Larger monitors do cost more, but for some types of work, they are almost essential.

Many of the new generation of portable or laptop computers use a screen called LCD (liquid crystal display), similar to what is used in popular watches. The LCD screen produces a high quality, clear display that makes it easy to view the screen even though it may be somewhat small.

CPU (CENTRAL PROCESSING UNIT)

The heart of the computer is the central processing unit, or the CPU. If the computer had a brain, this would be it. The CPU is a complex electronic circuit that is usually an integrated circuit or "chip." A computer chip is a tiny device, often smaller than one or two inches square and a fraction of an inch high, but it contains all the circuitry necessary to run the computer (bigger is not always better in computers).

Most of the activity takes place in the central processing unit, since the CPU is responsible for translating instructions into action. Almost all the instructions, commands, and results go through the CPU, at

phenomenally fast rates, like up to 90 MILLION actions
per second (that's 20,000 times faster than the blink of
an eye). I told you it is fast, remember? Although many
refer to the entire main computer box with all its internal
components as the "CPU", technically the CPU is the
main computer chip.

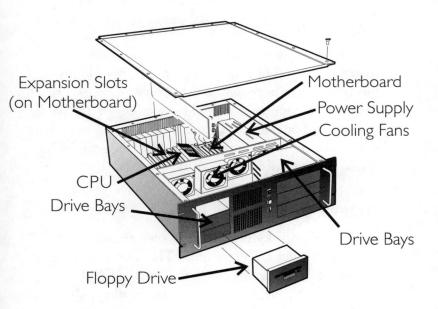

Expansion Slots
(on Motherboard)

Motherboard

Power Supply

Cooling Fans

CPU

Drive Bays

Drive Bays

Floppy Drive

Main Computer Unit

MEMORY

The computer keeps instructions and information in
a place called the memory. There are generally two types
of memory: ROM and RAM. ROM stands for Read
Only Memory. ROM is permanently installed in the
computer when it is made and cannot be changed or

erased. ROM contains information necessary for the operation of the computer.

RAM stands for Random Access Memory. Information and instructions in RAM can be changed or erased at any time, and anything put into this part of the memory is kept in RAM only as long as the computer is on.

HARD DISK

A hard disk is installed inside the computer and is used for storage of computer programs, files and other bits or pieces of information the computer needs. Data (that's the computer term for information) on the hard disk is saved or recorded by the computer and stays there even if the computer is turned off. The data can be erased from the disk, however, if necessary.

FLOPPY DISK DRIVE

A floppy disk drive is part of the computer into which you insert a "floppy" disk. The term *floppy* is used because at one time disks were thin and "floppy."

Although newer disks are smaller and covered with a firm plastic coating, many people still refer to all disks as "floppy." These disks may have programs recorded on them (such as programs you buy; these are called *program disks*), or they can have nothing on them (these are called *blank* disks) and thus are used to record data from the computer.

A floppy disk drive is necessary because most programs you buy must be loaded into the computer memory from disks. A floppy disk drive also provides a way to make extra copies of data you have entered and to use that copy on another computer. Many disks can be used on other computers of similar type, so you can, for example, make a copy of a document you have used on one computer and use it on another in a different location.

ARITHMETIC LOGIC UNIT

All mathematical calculations of a computer program are done in the arithmetic logic unit, or ALU. In most modern computers, this is built into the CPU. Any action that involves computation of numbers uses the ALU. This is not a simple calculator, but a unit which handles numbers using the binary (two) number system in a complex electronic manner that allows the ALU to do any type of calculation.

OTHER PARTS OF THE COMPUTER

The parts of the computer described so far are required for every computer, but many more computer accessories (called peripherals, peripheral devices or components) are also available to make your computer more useful, more productive, or just more fun to use. Some of these peripherals (you might as well get used to using computer terminology now) include:

PRINTER. If you want to have a paper copy of the computer output, you need a printer connected to your computer.

MOUSE. Not to be confused with the rodents of the same name. A computer mouse is so called because it somewhat resembles the rodent from which its name is taken. A computer mouse is used to control the direction of an arrow, bar, icon, or other item on the screen and

also allows you to select items on the screen by pointing to them and clicking on the mouse button. A mouse also allows you to scroll through text to move, copy or delete it and may be used as an alternative to pressing function keys to perform certain tasks.

MODEM. A modem is necessary to connect your computer to your telephone line for communication capabilities, such as accessing bulletin boards, online services, and database information services.

SPEAKERS. All personal computers come with a tiny built-in speaker. These speakers are primarily used to produce the "beeps" you hear to signal a problem or error, alert the user to the need for text entry, or to provide voice capabilities. If you want to have high quality sound for the increasingly popular multimedia programs on the market today, external speakers are necessary. These speakers may be similar to the type of speaker used for a hi-fi or stereo, but with a built-in amplifier.

CD-ROM (Compact Disk-Read Only Memory) **DRIVE.** A CD-ROM Drive allows the computer to use the huge amounts of data and programs on CD-ROM Disks.

SCANNER. A scanner converts pictures and drawings into a form the computer can use.

None of the peripherals or components described here is necessary for the operation of the computer, but some (or all) of them are commonly used with many computers. These peripherals provide many additional capabilities for computer use, and at the same time make using a computer more fun, more challenging and more rewarding. The majority of these peripherals are also available in portable versions as well as in full-size versions, so you can use a computer and all the peripheral devices you can carry (and afford) any time, any where.

The peripherals or components described here and the wires, extra keyboard keys, flashing characters, and speed of the actions create an aura of electronic wizardry that makes many people afraid to touch any part of a computer. But in spite of all its complex electronic inner workings, a computer is actually a very sturdy unit that can survive just about anything short of an attack with a sledgehammer (which you will probably be tempted to try occasionally).

There is no need to fear that you will cause a short circuit, explosion, fire, or any other damage to the computer by using the wrong keys, commands, or anything else you are likely to do. If you do touch the wrong key or use the wrong commands, the most common result will be that nothing will happen, or the computer will put out an error message, or you'll lose data or a program, or a 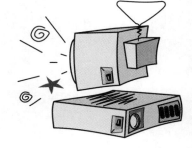 program will not run. While any of these results can be very frustrating for you, they won't hurt the computer.

Most computer programs will easily withstand wrong entries and the like. In addition, many programs will also can help you to discover the error by indicating what is wrong and then help further by giving you some clue as to the nature of the problem.

Problems are much more likely to originate from *lack* of use than from any type of use you can give the computer, and the very best way to avoid these problems is to use the computer regularly. The more you use your computer, the easier it will become to use, and the sooner you will learn to take control of one of the best—and fastest—helpers you've ever had.

CHAPTER 3

INSTRUCTIONS FOR THE COMPUTER
*If You Speak Its Language,
It Always Listens*

Once you have learned what a computer is, what it can do, and what its various components do, it is also helpful to learn something about how the computer works.

A computer will follow your instructions exactly—without hesitation, without question, as many times as you want, whenever you want. A computer never gets sick, never complains about anything, never becomes tired or bored, never takes a vacation or even a coffee break, and never expects anything in return for all its work. Sounds impossible, doesn't it? It isn't.

This kind of performance is available from any computer as long as you provide it with complete and precise instructions for what you want it to do. Remember, a computer does not think, reason, or make decisions on its own. *You* do all that, and the computer follows your instructions.

You provide these complete and precise instructions by using a program. A program is necessary because a computer only understands instructions that are entered in a complex computer language. A computer uses a special kind of program called a language translator to change your instructions into this computer language. What this all means is that you need a program so that you can enter information into a computer in a language you understand and have it translated into a language the computer understands.

A programming language is necessary because a computer works by comparing and changing the sequence of high voltage and low voltage, which can be represented by two numbers (zero and one) in the inner electronics of the computer. The comparing and changing all happens *very* rapidly (this is where those 100 million-per-second actions take place).

The right combination of a series of zeros and ones sets the sequence of events in motion to direct the computer to carry out instructions. The only way to put these numbers in the right sequence is to enter the information and instructions in the computer in machine language, which is the only language computers understand. But machine language is expressed like this:

00010001

00001001

10010000

11001010

Each one of these numbers is called a "bit " and each set of eight bits is called a "byte," and each byte represents only *one* letter, number or other character, so it could take a dozen or more of these lines to enter a single instruction!

As you can imagine, very few humans are able to use this complex and confusing machine language. So most people use a programming language, which allows them to enter the information and instructions into the computer in terms humans can understand and have the information and instructions translated into the machine language a computer understands.

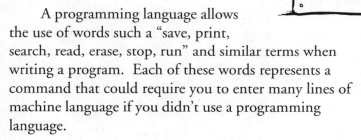

A programming language allows the use of words such a "save, print, search, read, erase, stop, run" and similar terms when writing a program. Each of these words represents a command that could require you to enter many lines of machine language if you didn't use a programming language.

There are many programming languages: BASIC, COBOL, FORTRAN, PASCAL, ADA, and ALGOL are just a few. These names may stand for the words that describe the type of programming language, or are a derivative of another name, or are named for a person.

For example, the name BASIC is taken from the first letters of its description: Beginners All-purpose Symbolic Instruction Code. BASIC is often the first programming language used by beginning programming students and is probably the most commonly used language. COBOL stands for COmmon Business Oriented Language and has a command structure that makes it suitable for business applications such as payroll, inventory, and accounting. FORTRAN stand for FORmula TRANslator and is used primarily for science and engineering purposes, since its command structure facilitates complex mathematical computations. ALGOL stands for ALGOrithmic Language and is used for scientific applications.

Ada and Pascal are programming languages named for people. Ada is named after Augusta Ada, the Countess of Lovelace, whose published examples of how an early computer design might be used are considered the first computer programs ever written. (You didn't think all the early computer work was done by men, did you?) Ada is a highly standardized programming language created for use by the Department of Defense for its many military computer applications.

Pascal is named for Blaise Pascal, a French mathematician and philosopher. Pascal is a structured computer language that must be written in a rigid format or structure in order to facilitate the understanding of how the program works .

These programming languages are all referred to as high-level languages, which means that they use simple English words to represent the various commands. By contrast, low-level languages, such as machine language, are more difficult to understand, and are generally used only by people who have more extensive computer knowledge.

Once a computer has the programming language built in or added, the computer still needs a program to do the specific task you want. The programming language is used *only* for translating instructions into machine code; you must also have a program for the specific task you want performed, such as a bookkeeping program to keep track of expenses, or an educational program to teach whatever course you have chosen, or an investment program to analyze your stocks and other investments, or a program that allows you to connect your computer to an online database or information service.

Computer programs commonly come on a disk or CD-ROM, but can also come in other formats, such as plug-in cartridges, for certain computers. The format of the program you use depends upon the computer you are using. But no matter what type of computer you are using, that computer will do nothing, except possibly flash a message like "floppy disk not ready " or "ready," or "OK," or "?" until it has a program. You can turn the computer on and the screen may light up and look as if it is ready to work, but nothing will happen (other than possibly the flashing of a message or symbol or character) until the computer has a program.

At one time, anyone who wanted to use a computer had to write his or her own program. Many people still enjoy writing computer programs, but writing a program that is capable of performing very many tasks not only requires knowledge of the general principles of computer programming, but also takes a fair amount of time as well (you can, however, write some simple programs that require very little knowledge of computer programming). These programs can help you understand how computer programs are written and 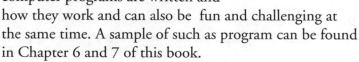 how they work and can also be fun and challenging at the same time. A sample of such as program can be found in Chapter 6 and 7 of this book.

If you do not know how to write a computer program or do not want to take the time to write one, you have four major sources for obtaining a program:

1. Buy one of the thousands of programs available for sale.

2. Use one of the thousands of shareware programs.

3. Use a public domain program.

4. Have someone write a program for you.

There are advantages and disadvantages to using each of these types of programs. These are some of these advantages and disadvantages you may want to consider when looking for a program:

PROGRAMS YOU BUY

Computer programs (don't forget, they're called *software)* available for sale may range from in price from $20-$30 or less to several hundred dollars. Cost does not necessarily reflect the quality, complexity, usefulness or support for the program. But, in many instances, the

higher the cost, the more a program can do. Many higher-priced programs not only contain more features, but also offer better instructions and documentation of these features.

The makers of some of these programs also provide technical support (in computer terminology, help is called support) if you have problems or if the program does not work properly. In addition, these programs are also more likely to be reviewed in computer magazines, so you can read about their features before buying them.

Another advantage to the higher-priced and more popular programs is that they often have a large base of established users, thus making it easier to find classes, books, videos and other instructional sources for learning to use all the features of the program. Help is also more likely to be available from SIGs (Special interest groups) or from other people who are using the program. The more popular programs are also more likely to have online help from either the maker of the program, from online help services, or from other users who enjoy helping fellow online users.

SHAREWARE

Shareware refers to programs that have been written by individuals or smaller companies who do not have the resources for large-scale marketing campaigns and who have chosen to distribute their programs on a try-before-you-buy basis. Some shareware programs are extremely useful and offer as many features as the higher-priced programs, while others may be lacking in some features and documentation.

Since these programs are usually not marketed in the traditional manner, it is sometimes more difficult to find complete information about their features. But many people use only shareware programs for both personal and business use and are completely satisfied with this type of program for all their computer needs.

Shareware programs allow users to try the program first and *then* pay for the program if they decide to use it. Prices for shareware programs are usually considerably less than for commercial programs, and anyone who buys these programs is on the honor system for paying the cost of the program if he or she decides to use it.

An added benefit of these programs is that it is often possible to talk directly to the people who wrote the program and find help from them. Shareware programs are available in some computer stores, from computer clubs or user groups, at computer fairs, libraries and schools, by mail order, and from online services.

PUBLIC DOMAIN PROGRAMS

Programs that may be used by anyone without charge or fear of infringement of copyrighted material are called *public domain* programs. Public domain programs are much like the shareware programs, except that no fee at all is charged for them, and users can often copy the program and give it away to other users. Public domain programs have the same advantages and disadvantages as the shareware programs, and can also be obtained from the same type of sources.

CUSTOM PROGRAMS

With the current availability of thousands of programs designed to do just about every task imaginable, very few individuals today find it necessary to have

someone write a custom program for their needs. Custom programs are generally written for highly specialized businesses or the rare specific circumstances where no other programs are available. Even for these special uses, people can often adapt or modify an existing program for their use.

When one person or a group of people write a program for a specific purpose, that person or group must provide all the instructions and technical support and also be available to make additions, changes and corrections to the program.

In addition to the expense and time involved in having a person or group write a program, all types of problems can occur when using a program that only a small number of people understand and support. So, while having a program written is one way to find a program for your needs, it is not an option very many people choose these days.

With all this in mind, how do you choose a program? In a word, *carefully*. As a computer user, you have a wide choice of what type of program you use, how much you pay for it, and where you get the program to do the work you want to do. The choice of program that is best for you depends entirely on your needs and circumstances.

Before you make the decision about what program to use, it is wise to check with other computer users or to visit computer stores, who often have demonstration copies of programs available for you to see and try. A visit to your library could also be very worthwhile. Many libraries have copies of computer magazines that carry reviews of programs. Most libraries also have books or videos about some of the programs. These books can often describe the features of the program and can also be a good source of help in learning or understanding it.

If you buy a program, you may also want to check the return policy for the store or mail order house. Some commercial programs are not returnable if you are not satisfied with the program, while others come with a return guarantee from the manufacturer or the store.

No matter what program you use or where you get the program, try to find out as much as you can about the program *before* you decide which one to use. Any program requires a certain amount of time to learn to use, whether you pay nothing or a little or a lot for it, and you won't want to spend that time on a program that does not suit your needs.

You may wonder why you can't just use someone else's program and save all the expense of buying a program. The reason you can't do this is that it is illegal to use a program (other than public domain or shareware) that you did not buy. Copying a program is like copying a book, a record, or anything else that is copyrighted. Yes,

people do it all the time, but that does not make it legal or right. You also cheat yourself out of free upgrades (new releases or corrections or additions to the program) if you copy a program from someone else. People who would not dream of stealing merchandise from a store sometimes think it is all right to copy programs, but the fact remains that it is illegal and a punishable crime to copy a computer program. *Please don't do it.*

Once you have decided on the program you need and have obtained a copy of it, you (or someone) needs to install the program on your computer. Some computers are sold with one or more programs already installed and ready to use. But in many instances, you must install a program (or have someone do it for you) on your computer.

Installing a program usually involves just inserting the disks for the program into your disk drive or accessing the program from your CD-ROM drive. Instructions for the installation usually appear on screen and are fairly straightforward. If you've never installed a program before, you may find it helpful or comforting to have a computer friend nearby for help if necessary.

If you are buying a new computer and a program or programs at the same time, many stores will install the programs for you.

Once the program is in place, the computer is ready to go to work. Some programs have all the instructions built in, are very easy to use, and are forgiving if you make a mistake. For some programs, however, you will need to learn some new terminology and how to follow those all-important instructions. For instance, pressing a key plus the letter "p" may be used as a command to print, or pressing the "home" key may mean to return to the beginning of the document. Some instructions in some programs may not be so easy to remember, however, and it may take time to learn that pressing a certain function key, such as F7, is the command to save or print.

The greatest difference in learning computer instructions and learning any other type of instructions is that computer instructions tend to be more precise and in many instances must be done in a specific order. Remember, you must provide those instructions to the computer in a manner it can understand and use. And, just as in cooking or driving or many other activities, if you follow the required procedures often enough, they become so automatic you hardly have to think about them.

Although the procedures required for using a computer are probably more detailed and more specific than those for anything else you have ever used, you'll soon discover that a computer carries out more detailed work than anything else you have ever used—and does it better, faster, and more accurately, too. If you practice regularly so that you develop familiarity with the computer, it will respond to your every command—promptly, accurately, and without question or complaint. Can anyone resist the temptation to have a response like that to his or her every instruction?

CHAPTER 4

A LITTLE BIT OF DOS
It's Ready to Work for You

All computers must have an operating system. If you're using an IBM compatible computer, the computer uses a *disk operating system*, or DOS. DOS is a collection of programs that controls the flow of information, programs and the various parts of the computer system. DOS loads programs (software) that run on the computer, organizes the information that the computer uses, and carries out tasks such as displaying information on the screen, reading and writing information on disks, and managing printers.

You could think of DOS as being like the manager of a busy airport. The airport manager sees to it that the control tower directs all incoming and outgoing flights to the correct runways, that all the baggage and passengers are directed to the correct areas to leave on flights or pick up baggage, and that the airport is kept in good order.

DOS does the same sort of management tasks on your computer.

While you don't need to know everything about DOS in order to use it, learning a few basics about DOS  will help you to take advantage of some of its features. You use DOS to load software in your computer by entering a few letters at the DOS prompt to indicate which program you want to load. DOS takes care of finding the program and loading the program and then turning control of the computer to that program, which is known as running the program.

The DOS prompt is usually the first and only thing to appear on your computer screen when you turn it on. The DOS prompt looks like this:

C:>   or   C:\>

You may use a computer where a different letter appears, or someone may have set up DOS to display a menu or another special display, but on most computers you'll see the DOS prompt as shown above when you turn the computer on. The prompt indicates DOS is loaded in memory and is waiting for you to enter a command.

You also use DOS to do what are called "maintenance" or "housekeeping" tasks. These tasks are similar to the usual types of maintenance or housekeeping tasks you do for your home, apartment or room; that is, organizing items and keeping them in order and getting rid of unwanted and unused items. DOS is considerably less strenuous than the housekeeping tasks you use at home— and much more challenging and interesting.

You can use DOS to do the many types of tasks on your disk. You do these tasks by entering commands at the DOS prompt. DOS is not case sensitive, so you may enter these commands in upper or lower case, or a combination of both. After you enter the command, you must press **ENTER** to have the command carried out. Here are some DOS commands and what they do:

TIME: Displays the system time on your computer. If the time is incorrect, you may enter the correct time. The time is important because it will be displayed with files that are saved.

DATE: Displays the system date on your computer. If the date is incorrect, you may enter the correct date. The date is important because it will be displayed with files that are saved.

DIR: Short for Directory. This command displays a list of the files on the default directory (the directory shown at the DOS prompt). You may change to another directory to see a list of files on whatever directory you want.

CLS: Short for Clear Screen. Used to clear the screen of all data.

COPY: Used to copy, or duplicate, a file. Files can be copied from one disk or directory to the same disk or directory, or to another disk or directory. Copies can be assigned the same name only when copied to another disk or directory, or they may be given a new name.

DEL: Short for Delete. Used to erase or delete files from disk.

ERASE: Erases or deletes a file. Similar to DEL.

REN: Short for Rename. Used to change the name of an existing file.

TYPE: Displays the contents of a listable disk file.

VER: Short for Version. Displays the version number of DOS you are using. There are several versions of DOS, somewhat like the volumes of a magazine; the higher the number, the later the version.

PATH: Used to list the "path" of the directories on your computer; that is the order in which the computer will search directories to find the information or programs you've requested.

MD: Abbreviation for Make Directory. Used to create a subdirectory on your disk.

RD: Abbreviation for Remove Directory. Used to remove a directory or subdirectory from your disk.

CD: Abbreviation for Change Directory. Used to change from the current directory to another directory.

CHAPTER 5

SHOPPING FOR A COMPUTER:
You're Still in Charge if You Know What the Ads Really Say

S hopping for a computer or just trying to understand the features of a computer you're using can be very confusing, especially with all the new terms used to describe computers and their accessories.

Some of these terms have developed because of the technology brought about by computers, but many of them are nothing more than "computerese," or the lingo that computer users tend to attach to anything associated with a computer.

"Computerese" can be very intimidating, particularly to someone new to this type of technology. But don't let "computerese" scare you—it is nothing more than a jargon that has developed with the increased use of computers, and it is no different from the jargon associated with many business, hobby, sports or other activities.

If you put forth a little effort, you can learn to understand the language of computers and begin to use it like a "pro." And understanding the language of computers will definitely keep you in charge when shopping for a computer or learning to use one you already have at home or work.

Before shopping for a computer, you should give some thought to the type of computer you need, want and can afford. Shopping will be easier if you think about the first two questions that most computer sales people will (or should) ask you: what will you use the computer to do and do you want an IBM or compatible or a Macintosh computer. (Some sales people may use computer terms to ask these questions. For example, asking what "applications" you are planning to run means what type software are you planning to use; asking what "platform" are you interested in using means do you want IBM or compatible or Macintosh).

One point to consider when deciding between an IBM or compatible or Macintosh is whether you use one of these types at work or school and whether you want to have the same type of computer at home. If that is not the case, then thinking about the type of use you plan for your computer and the software you will use to do that work may help with your decision.

The type of work you do will help determine whether you need to buy a computer that is well suited for extensive calculations, for graphics, sound and/or multimedia capabilities, for business applications, word processing, desktop publishing, or any other needs.

The technology and price structure for IBM or compatible and Macintosh is quite different. Macintosh computers tend to be more expensive and are often used by those who work primarily with graphic images. IBM or compatible computers usually cost less and are more widely used for business and personal use. Since IBM or compatibles tend to be more popular, you are likely to find more programs written for these computers.

Other questions you're likely to be asked are whether you need a computer that's portable, how much you will use the computer, and possibly how much you plan to spend. If you need a portable computer (they're called laptop computers these days), you can find one that has just about everything available in desktop versions, but you will have different options if you need a smaller notebook or the even smaller palmtop computer.

The amount of time you spend using your computer can help determine the amount of disk space you'll need, the speed of the computer, and the type of monitor to buy. Other factors may enter into your decision about what type of computer to buy, but thinking about these points will help you decide on the options available.

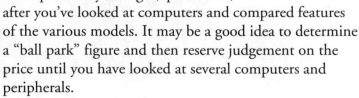

You need to think about the amount of money you will be able to spend on a computer, but you may not want to reveal the amount to salespeople. The amount you spend on a computer may change (up or down) after you've looked at computers and compared features of the various models. It may be a good idea to determine a "ball park" figure and then reserve judgement on the price until you have looked at several computers and peripherals.

One good way to determine what type of computer you'll want and how much you spend is to browse through computer advertising in newspapers and magazines to see what is available in the marketplace. One look at some computer advertising is enough to bring out the computer fears in anyone, but if you learn some computer terminology and then learn something about each feature, the information can be very helpful in selecting the type of computer, peripherals, and programs you'll buy.

These are some terms you're likely to see in a computer ad:

THE COMPUTER:

- Multimedia Computer (or Multimedia Built In)
- Intel 486 DX2/66Mhz processor
    (or Pentium 90 MHz)
    (or Motorola 68LC040 66 MHz Microprocessor)
- 4 (8, 12, 16 or more) MB RAM
    or 2 MB Memory Expandable
    to 32 MB
- 270 (or 420, 720, 1275) MB hard drive
    Double Speed (or Quad Speed) CD-ROM drive
- 16-bit stereo sound card
- Stereo speakers
- Fax/modem (or 14.4 bps fax modem)
    or 9600/2400 fax/modem
- 6 expansion slots
- 5 storage bays

- Built-in telephone answering system
- 1 MB local bus video
- MS-DOS 3.1 (or 5.0, 6.0, or similar)
- Built in Serial and Parallel Ports
- Mini Tower
- Keyboard and Two-Button Mouse Included
- 3.5" Floppy drive
- Pre-loaded software

MONITOR:

- 14" RGB Monitor
- 14" SVGA Monitor
        .28 (or .39) dot pitch

LASER PRINTER:

- 300 dpi
- 4 ppm print speed
- 8 (16, 24, 26 or more)
        scalable typefaces
- PCL5 printer language
- 1 MB memory

INKJET PRINTER:

- 250 cps draft
- 8 fonts

NOTEBOOK COMPUTER:

- 8.4 active matrix color display
  or Lcd screen
- PCMCIA Slot

Let's look at each of these features and see what these ads tell you:

COMPLETE MULTIMEDIA PACKAGE (OR MULTIMEDIA BUILT IN)

The term "multimedia" does not actually refer to a computer device or peripheral, but to the capabilities of a computer to combine graphics, sound and visual displays. When a computer is advertised with "multimedia built in" or as a "complete multimedia package," that computer

 usually comes with speakers and enough memory and disk space to run multimedia software from CD-ROMs or other disks.

By using multimedia software on a computer that can run that software, you can listen to music on the computer speakers and at the same time see the music displayed on the screen (or see the musicians playing the music, or see any type of moving or still images) *and* hear a voice describing what is happening. High quality multimedia computers allow you to use a computer program to play a scene from a movie, see and hear interviews with the stars of the movie and to select questions and then see and hear the actors' response to those questions.

Multimedia programs allow you to watch lions roaming in their native Africa, hear the lions' sounds and listen to a description of the lions' habitat—all at the same time. Multimedia software programs allow you to watch and hear the speeches of dignitaries, presidents, and scientists (or anyone whose speech has been made available on multimedia software), to watch and hear NASA spaceships launched, and to see and hear events that at one time you could only read about or see on television or in movies.

Multimedia programs allow you use your computer very much like television or movies—but multimedia goes one step further because it is *interactive*, which means that *you* can choose what part of the program you see, when to stop and start, and in which order the program will run. Multimedia programs can be used for education or entertainment, and business, and are among the most popular uses for computers today.

Multimedia programs do require faster computers, more memory and additional sound capabilities, but they will also make your computer considerably more useful for the whole family. If you're planning to use your computer for multimedia programs, it's even more critical to know as much as you can about computers before you shop. And—you probably guessed this one already—a computer with multimedia capabilities is going to cost more.

486DX/2 66MHZ (OR 486SX/4)

The 486DX/SX/2 refers to the microprocessor, or chip, and the 486 indicates the "model" computer chip. These models are somewhat like car models in that they tell the era and design of the chip. The earlier chips were called the 8086 and 8088, then came the 286, 386 and now the 486 and Pentium. The Pentium is the most recent model chip (at this moment), and if the numbering sequence had been followed, it would be called a 586.

DX (OR SX):

This indicates whether the chip contains the complete set of computer instructions (the "DX"), or a limited set of computer instructions (the "SX"). The SX chip does not mean that the computer won't run well because it is lacking in instructions. To use the car analogy again, you might think of the SX as being like a compact car and the DX like a full-size car: they'll both take you where you want to go, but the compact car may not be able to reach speeds of 100 miles per hour and it may not have the power or the special features of the full-size car.

The /2 or /4 refers to the ability of the chip to internally double (/2) or quadruple (/4) the native computer clock speed.

25 (OR /50/60/90) MHZ

These numbers tell you the native clock speed of the computer. MHZ stands for *megahertz*, or million cycles per second. The higher the number, the faster the computer will process information.

MOTOROLA 68LCO40 66 MHZ MICROPROCESSOR

This describes a chip commonly used in the Apple Macintosh computers, and the numbers indicate the model of the chip, just as they do in the IBM compatible computers.

8 (OR 12, 16 OR MORE) MB RAM

RAM stands for Random Access Memory, and the "MB" stands for megabytes, or million bytes (remember that a byte is a computer unit of storage). The total number of bytes available indicates the amount of space the computer has available for carrying out its tasks, such as storing data and instructions and running programs.

Computers that have larger amounts of memory will usually cost more, since the additional memory requires additional memory "chips." A computer with 8 MB of RAM is probably adequate for most personal computer use, but much depends on what kinds of software you plan to use with the computer.

Some software requires a certain minimum amount of memory, so it is helpful to decide what types of software you are likely to use and then check to be sure the computer you are considering has enough memory to run this software.

2 MB MEMORY EXPANDABLE TO 32 MB

Memory that can be expanded means that additional segments of memory can be added to the computer at a later time to increase the memory up to 32 MB. This feature can be important if you want to keep the initial cost of the computer down, or are uncertain about the amount of memory you'll need, or want to be sure the memory can be expanded if you need it to accommodate other software or larger amounts of data at a later time.

270 (OR MORE) MB HARD DRIVE

The hard drive is where software and data files are stored, so the larger the hard drive, the more space you have for software and for data you want to store on your hard drive. The amount of space is measured in million bytes, or MB.

DOUBLE, DUAL OR QUAD SPEED CD-ROM

CD-ROM stands for Compact Disk-Read Only Memory. A CD-ROM disk looks much like an audio CD-ROM but contains computer software as well as accompanying sound, pictures, text, and graphics. A CD-ROM is commonly used as part of multimedia software because it holds large amounts of data in many forms. A single CD-ROM can contain an entire encyclopedia, including the text, pictures, sounds, graphics and anything else associated with each entry. A CD-ROM player is built in to many computers today or one can be added to a computer, either inside the computer or as a separate box outside.

CD-ROMs can be played at several speeds: regular, double, triple or quadruple. The faster the speed, the faster the data is read from the disk. For example, a movie clip contained in multimedia software needs to be read at a speed fast enough to keep it from appearing "jerky" on the screen. A CD-ROM playing at double speed is usually able to do this. A double speed CD-ROM player can also spin the CD-ROM disks at either regular or double speed, and a quadruple speed CD-ROM player can spin them at all the speeds. A "quad" speed CD-ROM player is currently considerably more expensive, and some software is not designed for use at these speeds.

16 BIT SOUND CARD

A sound card (a card is a flat circuit board that fits into one of the slots inside the computer) translates computer instructions into sound, such as speech, music, etc. The "16 bit" indicates the amount of information that is received at one time. Sound cards receive information at 8, 16 or 32 bits at a time. This information somewhat compares to the way cars travel on road with various number of lanes: more cars could travel on 8 lanes than on 4, and more on 4 than on 2 lanes. The number of bits received by the sound card translates into sound quality, and more is better. That is, 32 bits produces better sound than 16, and 16 produces better than 8.

STEREO SPEAKERS

Stereo speakers for a computer are similar to ones used in a home or car stereo system, but generally require a built-in amplifier. Speakers that come with computers are generally compact to fit on a desk with the computer. Since an amplifier is required with these speakers, the speakers need to be plugged into an outlet in addition to being connected to the computer.

FAX/MODEM (OR 14.4 BPS OR 9600/2400 FAX MODEM)

A modem is a device that connects your computer to your telephone line and then can be used to connect your computer to online services such as the Internet, Active color matrix, Prodigy, Compuserve, and others.

A fax modem can also send documents directly from your computer to other standard fax machines (fax is an abbreviation for facsimile) or other computers equipped with a fax modem. You'll also need software that has fax modem capabilities to send documents this way. Once you have the fax modem and the software installed and working, this feature can save you hours of time if you send many documents via fax. When you fax directly from a computer, you no longer have to print out a document, take it to the fax machine, put the document in the fax, enter the fax number, and send the fax. All this is done by selecting the options on your computer. Some software has options so that you can automate the process and use one command to send a fax to several people, or send faxes during times when rates are lower, and so forth.

The 14.4 bps refers to the rate of transmission of data, expressed as bps, or bits per second. The number 14.4 is short for 14,400 bps and is commonly used today, but 28.8 (short for 28,800) is rapidly becoming more popular. These numbers refer to modems only; the fax modem is limited by current standards to 9600 bps. The higher the number, the more data is transmitted in a given amount of time.

If a fax/modem is listed as 9600/2400 bps, the fax transmits at 9600 bps and the modem at 2400 bps.

6 EXPANSION SLOTS

Expansion slots are used for adding cards that allow you to use additional features with your computer, such as sound, more memory, fax modems, scanners, specialized video display, and so forth. Cards are available in several varieties: ISA, EISA, PCI, MCA, and PCMCIA (which are used with laptops and described in that section). These initials refer to various standards that have evolved, each one providing additional features that may not have been available previously. Briefly, the newer slots (PCI, MCA) provide faster data transfer (for example, 32 bits rather than 16 bits) and extra control features.

5 STORAGE BAYS

Storage bays are empty spots in the computer where you can put various additional devices, such as extra hard drives, tape backup devices, CD-ROM drives, etc. The number of bays usually refers to the total number of bays in the computer, and some of these bays may already have been used by devices already installed.

BUILT IN TELEPHONE ANSWERING SYSTEM

If a computer has a built in telephone answering system, the computer has software that allows you to use a modem to receive telephone messages. Some telephone answering systems have extensive capabilities for receiving messages, such as calling number recognition, selective messages capabilities, and so forth. A note to consider: if you want to use a telephone answering system with your computer, your computer must be running at all times you plan to use this option.

1 MB LOCAL BUS VIDEO

A local bus video speeds the transmission of information to be displayed on the monitor. If you're using multimedia software, the speed of the display is especially important to avoid seeing jerky moves when watching video or movie clips. The 1 MB refers to the amount of memory in local bus video.

MS/DOS 6.2 OPERATING SYSTEM

These letters are designations for the most popular operating systems found in most personal computers. The operating system is the principal controlling program of the computer. It directs the computer in the operation of any input or output devices, such as the keyboard, printer, and disk drives.

MS/DOS stands for Microsoft Disk operating system. MS is a trademark of Microsoft Corp. MS/DOS is used in IBM compatible computers. The registered IBM version of MS/DOS is called PC-DOS or IBM-DOS.

The 6.2 identifies the version of the operating system, much like the edition of a magazine; the higher the number, the more recent the version. Some programs require a certain version (or later) of the operating system.

WINDOWS is currently a popular form of an operating system and can run with DOS or in addition to it. Windows allows the use of icons, or graphic images, to access and use the various features of the operating system.

MINI TOWER

A mini tower means that the computer cabinet is designed to be placed vertically rather than horizontally. A vertical cabinet somewhat resembles a tower, and thus its name. A mini tower is shorter than a standard tower.

KEYBOARD AND TWO-BUTTON MOUSE INCLUDED

A keyboard and mouse are usually included in the price of the computer these days. Most keyboards include a standard typewriter-style keyboard, a set of function keys, and a separate calculator-style number pad for those who are used to using a calculator for entering numbers.

A "mouse" is a small device that's connected to the computer with a cord and that somewhat resembles the rodent for which is named. A mouse sits on the desktop or on a small pad and is guided by your hand. Moving the mouse moves a pointer or cursor on the screen and allows you to enter the designated information by clicking a mouse button. A mouse can have one or two buttons; a two-button mouse allows you to access different features included with some programs. The usual mouse is designed for use by a right-handed person, but a left-handed mouse is also available.

3.5" FLOPPY DISK DRIVE

A floppy disk drive is pretty standard on most computers at this time, and the 3.5" is the most commonly used size today. A floppy disk drive allows you to use disks to load programs into the computer and to save data on a disk. Although many programs can now be loaded into the computer from a CD-ROM, some programs are available on disks only.

A floppy disk drive is also used as a quick and easy way to make copies of data from your computer so that you have that information available as a backup, to take anywhere, or to use on another compatible computer.

PRE-LOADED SOFTWARE

If a computer is pre-loaded with software, certain software is installed and ready to use, and the cost of the software is included in the price of the computer. This option has both advantages and disadvantages. The advantages are that pre-loaded software saves you the time because you won't have to install the software and saves you money because you don't have to buy the software separately.

The disadvantage to pre-loaded software is that the software may not be what you need or will use. In addition, the software may take up disk space you may want to have available for other software. One alternative to buying a computer with pre-loaded software is to negotiate to have the store install the software *you* want as part of the purchase price of your computer.

An important point to consider with pre-loaded software is that some stores may not want to include the instruction manuals or original program disks for the software. Instruction manuals are invaluable sources of information about software, and it is important to have manuals for any software you own. Original program disks are necessary if you have to re-install the software at any time in the future. And finally, you need to have the registration number for all software so that you can register your copy and become eligible for upgrades and support from the manufacturer.

If you buy a computer with pre-loaded software, be sure that you also get instruction manuals, original disks and the registration cards for all the software.

MONITORS:

14" (or 15") .39 (or .28) RGB
   or SGVA Color Monitor

A 14" monitor measures 14" diagonally and this or the 15" size is currently the size used with many computers running multimedia software. Larger monitors offer more viewing area, but are considerably more expensive and also weigh more. For example, a 21" monitor can cost $800 to $1,000 or more and weigh 90 pounds.

The .39 refers to the resolution of the monitor. The smaller the number, the better the resolution. A monitor with .39 resolution is good, but .28 is better.

Resolution refers to the clarity of the picture on the monitor. Resolution can be important if you need to look at the monitor for long periods of time or see the detail in graphic or other detailed designs or in video or movie clips.

RGB stands for red-green-blue color monitor. A RGB color monitor has separate connections for each of the colors and therefore produces clearer and more brilliant colors on the monitor.

SVGA stands for Super Video Graphics Adapter. A VGA monitor is a high resolution monitor, and a super VGA monitor offers even higher resolution.

BUILT-IN SERIAL AND PARALLEL PORTS

A port is a socket on the computer and is used to connect the computer to various input or output devices such as a printer or a modem. Serial and parallel refer to the manner in which the information is transmitted or received through the ports.

Most printers require a computer with a parallel port, and most modems require a serial port, so a computer with both serial and parallel ports is likely to be essential if you plan to use a printer and a modem with your computer.

Ports can be built in or added as an option and you can have more than one. Like all other accessories, ports must be compatible with the specific computer you are using.

PRINTERS (LASER, INKJET, AND DOT MATRIX)

LASER

- 300 dpi
- 4 ppm print speed
- 26 Scalable Typefaces
- PCL5 Printer Language
- 1 MB Memory
- 64K (or 1 MB Buffer)

LASER PRINTER

A laser printer produces high quality printing that gives documents a clean, professional look. The quality of print from a laser printer can be good enough to be used as a master copy that is used by a printer for newsletters, brochures and the like.

300 DPI

Characters printed by a laser printer are formed with a series of dots that are extremely close together. The more dots used to form the character, the more precise the character appears. The most popular laser printers today usually print 300 dpi, or dots per inch. Laser printers that produce copy at 600, 1200 and 1800 dpi are available for those who need better printouts.

Most laser printers can print on 8½ x 11" paper, but models are available that will also print on the larger 11 x 17" size paper. Many laser printers can also print envelopes.

4 PPM PRINT SPEED

Laser printers produce copy at varying rates of speed. A print speed of 4 ppm (pages per minute) is one of the slower speeds; recent models can print 8, 10 and 12 or more pages per minute.

26 SCALABLE TYPEFACES

Scalable typefaces allow you to print text in the stated number of different typefaces (some people refer to them as fonts), and scalable means that they can be printed in any size. Some printers allow the addition of more typefaces so that you have a greater selection of typefaces and sizes.

PCL5 PRINTER LANGUAGE

PCL5 stands for Printer Control Language, version 5, and is the page description language used by Hewlett Packard, one of the larger companies producing printers.

1 MB MEMORY

1 MB of memory indicates the amount of memory in the laser printer. The amount of memory is important because text, graphics and characters are stored here while being processed for printing. If the printer does not have enough memory for the work you are doing, the printing process may be slowed down.

64K (OR 1 MB) BUFFER

Most computers transmit information much faster than it can be printed on most printers, and a buffer provides a place to dump (more computer jargon, meaning "to put in") information from the computer. This information can then be printed at whatever speed the printer uses, and you can go on and use the computer for some other task without having to wait for the printer to finish.

The numbers indicate the size of the buffer and reflect the amount of data that can be stored for printing.

INKJET PRINTER

- 250 cps Draft
- 8 Fonts

An inkjet printer produces characters by means of tiny inkjets that form dots on the page. The quality of the print from an inkjet printer varies greatly, depending upon the printer. An inkjet printer is usually faster than a laser printer and also uses less energy. In addition, inkjet printers that produce color print are usually considerably less expensive than color laser printers.

250 CPS DRAFT

An inkjet printer that prints 250 cps (characters per second) will print faster than a dot matrix printer. Inkjet printers also may list the dpi output of their printer as well, and this is usually similar to what a laser printer produces.

8 FONTS

An inkjet printer that prints 8 fonts (or typefaces) has this number of fonts available for printing text. Inkjet printers can also print graphics as well. The combination of graphics and color printing from an inkjet printer allows users to produce colorful documents that can be very appealing.

DOT MATRIX PRINTER

A dot matrix printer uses a series of tiny dots to form each character. Some of the dot matrix printers have a "near letter quality" (or correspondence quality) mode to make the print more readable and less dot-like. Dot matrix printers are the usually the least expensive type you can buy and are the only type that can easily print out multipart forms.

NOTEBOOK (OR LAPTOP, PALMTOP, OR ANY PORTABLE COMPUTER):

- LCD screen or Active Matrix Color Display
- PCMCIA Slot

LCD SCREEN OR ACTIVE MATRIX COLOR DISPLAY

LCD stands for Liquid Crystal Display, a type of screen commonly used for notebook or palmtop computers. A liquid crystal display is similar to the type used on the face of a digital watch, but on a much bigger scale. The display tends to have poor contrast and is not as clear as the display on a standard television or CRT (cathode ray tube) monitor, but is suitable for portable computers because it uses less current.

An active matrix color display means that the screen has a crisper, brighter, higher quality display and costs more than a passive matrix display. If you're considering a laptop or palmtop computer, you'll need to see the different types of displays to decide which type of screen is best for your needs.

PCMCIA SLOT

A PCMCIA slot is designed especially for use in laptops because of its compact design. PCMCIA stands for Personal Computer Memory Card International Association. A PCMCIA slot is used to plug in various cards, about the size of a credit card, to add extra features such as modems, extra hard drives, additional memory, network adapters, and so forth.

What you have just read is a sampling of some of the many computer terms you may see listed in advertising or read about in computer magazines. There are many others, but these are some of the more common ones.

Once you have learned some computer terminology, have some general idea of the types of uses you plan for your computer and what types of programs you are likely to run on it, you are ready to look at computers.

Shopping for computers and accessories can be fun, and can also be a mind-boggling, interesting experience— all at the same time! It is fun to see the huge assortment of computers and accessories available; it is mind-boggling because of the number of items available and what they can do; and interesting to deal with computer salespeople.

Many computer salespeople are extremely knowl- edgeable and cooperative and can be very helpful in selecting a computer to suit your needs. But so many new computer products are developed and introduced that it is difficult for anyone to keep up with all the changes and advancements in this field, and you may find salespeople who are not aware of some of the newer software, peripherals, or even some of the newer computers on the market.

But the field of computers is also fiercely competi- tive, and computer salespeople today are often very knowledgeable about what is available in computers, peripherals and software.

So, shop for a computer much as you would shop for a car: learn all you can before hand, visit the showrooms, talk to the salespeople, look at all the options available, compare the prices, and check out the service and support.

When shopping for a computer, don't be afraid to ask lots of questions, and do expect reasonable replies. Remember, there are *no* dumb questions, only dumb answers.

"Try before you buy" applies to computer shopping just as it does for other shopping. Ask for a demonstration of the computer and all the peripherals that interest you.

You should be able to have a demonstration of how to connect any peripherals and how they work, and you should also be able to try using any computer and peripherals before you buy them.

Many computer stores include free lessons or seminars with a purchase, or they may offer other types of assistance to help you with your computer. The price of the computer, the options that are included with the commuter, and the service and support (help) from your computer dealer are very important.

Many computer stores offer on-site setup and support, or telephone support or in-store support and repair service. If you're a new computer user, it's especially important to find out what type of help is available if you have problems with the computer. The best price in town won't mean much if you have to send your computer across the country for repair—and then wait for several weeks for the repair to be completed.

Another important part of computer shopping is checking the user manual or documentation for the computer and peripherals. A computer that seems perfect for all your needs may lose some of its appeal after you discover that the user's manual is the size of an encyclopedia and the instructions are about as clear as Sanskrit. The documentation for any computer and peripherals should be reasonably concise, readily understandable, and contain instructions for all its uses. Otherwise, you may miss out on many uses for the computer just because the instructions are too complex, too vague, or not included at all (the latter does happen, surprisingly!).

The price of a computer may be higher at a computer store than it is from a mail order or discount store, but the amount of service and support available from a computer dealer could more than make up for the price difference. If lessons or other introductory services are included in the purchase price, buying from a computer store may be the most cost-effective way to fulfill your computer needs.

You may, however, be able to get some excellent prices on computers at a discount store or mail order house and then find support through courses available in your area, from friends, or from local user groups (computer owners who share common interests form clubs and meet regularly to discuss computer-related topics).

The choice of the computer that best serves your needs and the place where you buy a computer and peripherals is something only you can determine after considering the amount of money you have to spend, the type and amount of use you plan for the computer, and the importance of the options available with the computer.

Computers are available to suit just about any need and price range, from the smaller inexpensive models that have limited capabilities to the multipurpose computers that will do just about any task you need done.

You can learn a lot by shopping for a computer: you can watch demonstrations of the many tasks a computer can perform, see how easy it can be to use a computer, and discover the wide variety of programs and accessories available for a computer. And if you learn enough about computers beforehand, shopping for a computer can be an experience you'll enjoy—and that will still keep you in charge.

CHAPTER 6

NOW IT'S YOUR TURN
You Can Really Use a Computer

Now that you know a little about a computer and how it works, you may be interested to see how a computer program is written and how it is used in the computer. You could use a program forever without ever knowing how a program is written, and you may not care anything about how a program runs. If that is the case, you could easily skip over these next two chapters and still be able to use a computer to do everything described in earlier chapters of this book—and more.

But if you decide to learn a little about computer programs, you'll see why certain tasks can easily be done on a computer and others are very difficult to do. You'll also have an better idea of what is involved in programming, and this should help you decide whether or not you would like to go on to learn more.

The next two chapters introduce you to some of the terminology used to write a program and show you how the computer uses the commands in a program. These chapters include a demonstration of how a simple program is written, then put into the computer, and then run in the computer.

These parts of a program are three separate processes, somewhat like the process of making a cake. First, you decide what kind of cake you'll make and find a recipe for that cake; then, you assemble the ingredients and put them together in the right order; and then, you put the cake in the oven to bake.

You use the same process for a computer program: first, you design and write the program; then, you put the program into the computer; and then, you have the computer run the program.

A very simple program could contain just one line, such as:

```
10    PRINT "Name"
```

Believe it or not, that one line does constitute a computer program. But when that program runs, the only task it will perform is to put the word "Name" on the screen or printout. This program doesn't show you very much about the computer or its many capabilities.

But, by using a program that contains several lines, I can demonstrate a program which could be very useful in many ways and that also illustrates much more of what the computer can do. I will list a short program and then explain it line by line.

The strange-looking characters are not as complicated as they look; they are just part of the BASIC programming language, and they will soon be as easy to understand as the other abbreviations and terms you have been using for years.

Ready? Here goes . . .

Suppose you want to keep a list of people and their addresses, and then separate the people on this list according to the type of membership or association they have with a group. A program in BASIC to set up the format for doing this would look like this on most computers:

```
10    REM A SIMPLE PROGRAM IN
      BASIC; ADDRESS FILE
20    PRINT "NAME";
30    INPUT N$
40    PRINT "STREET ADDRESS";
50    INPUT SA$
60    PRINT "CITY, STATE, ZIP";
70    INPUT C$
80    PRINT "TYPE: 1 JUNIOR, 2 SENIOR
      3 FAMILY";
90    INPUT T
100   PRINT "THE ENTRY IS"
110   PRINT N$
120   PRINT SA$
130   PRINT C$
```

```
140     PRINT T
150     END
```

Each entry in *each* of the lines above has a specific purpose, and some of the punctuation marks are also computer commands as well. When all these commands are put together in a program, they provide the computer with those complete and precise instructions described in the previous chapters.

As I explain each line, you'll see what I mean:

```
10      REM A SIMPLE PROGRAM IN
        BASIC; ADDRESS FILE
```

The "10" is the *line number*, which must be assigned at the beginning of each line of a BASIC program. When the program runs, the computer interprets the instructions one line at a time, in numeric order. Any number can be assigned to each line, but the first line of instruction must have the lowest number, the following line the next highest, and so on. You could number the lines 39, 47, 62, and so on, but using even numbers is just simpler.

The line numbers begin with one and increase by one for each line up to the capacity of the BASIC language you are using. The lines in this program are numbered 10, 20, 30, and so on, in order to have extra lines between commands for inserting additional instructions later.

REM stands for *remarks* and is sometimes written REMarks. This command indicates to the computer that whatever follows on this line will not be part of the program when it runs. REMarks lines are simply a record of what the program is, how it works, how you want identified, or any other comments to help you or any others who use the program.

REMarks can be put on several lines if necessary and may also be used elsewhere in the program for additional information, but each REMark line must have REM (or REMark) at the beginning of the line, no matter where it appears in the program.

REM   A SIMPLE PROGRAM IN BASIC;
ADDRESS FILE

This part of the line is just the way I chose to identify this program in the remark line. When you start writing programs, this is where you can add your name, date and other details, including a copyright if you wish, to identify your program. That will come later. Now back to this program:

The next line is:

20   PRINT "NAME";

The "20" is the line number and we have already discussed that. PRINT indicates to the computer that what follows inside the quotation marks should be printed out or shown on the screen, depending on the type of computer you are using. These quotation marks are one of the many punctuation marks that will have an entirely different use in computer programming. Quotation marks in a computer program are often used to indicate what is to be printed out and are not related in any way to the quotation marks used in writing.

When the program is run, any combination of letters, symbols, and numbers enclosed within the quotation marks will be printed out exactly as they appear on the programming line (The print command may be slightly different from the one shown here and could be something like a letter or symbol to indicate "print").

The semicolon after the quotation mark is another punctuation mark that has a different meaning in computer programming, and its use here also breaks the rules of grammar to follow the rules for instructions for the computer. The semicolon indicates to the computer that the cursor (a marker, sometimes invisible, that keeps track of where you are on the print line or on the screen) should stay where it is until the next command.

If you don't put the semicolon here, the cursor will automatically move to the next line after printing the word NAME when the program runs. Since the next command (INPUT N$) instructs the computer to put a question mark on the screen, the semicolon is used to indicate that the question mark should appear immediately after "NAME" rather than on the next line.

30   INPUT N$

INPUT indicates to the computer that information will be coming from the keyboard and that the computer should stop and wait for this information before continuing to the next lint of the program. The "input" command also signals the computer to put a question mark on the screen or paper, to let you know it is ready and waiting for you (or someone) to enter a response.

Since the computer follows your directions exactly, it will wait patiently for hours, or days if it has to, for this information (providing the power is kept on).

N$ is a way to indicate to the computer that the information coming from the keyboard will be letters, numbers, symbols, or combinations of these. I chose the letter "N" to indicate "NAME," but it could be any letter of the alphabet (or letters, depending upon the type of BASIC you are using).

The "$" next to the "N" means "string," or that a "string," or group, of characters will follow. This combination of a letter or letters and the "$" is called a *string variable*. Variables are part of the computer language you should understand, so please bear with me while I digress and explain what they are.

The computer must have a way to store all the information entered with a program, recall the information whenever needed, and have all the information identified or labeled. *Variables* allow you to do all this in a program. Whenever you put a variable in the program, the computer creates and reserves a space in memory for storing information and then identifies or labels the reserved space with whatever name you give it. You could change the information you put into this storage space with another command, but the space remains labeled with N$ (or whatever name you gave it) though the information in the space may vary; thus the name "variable."

> # String Variable?
> # Sounds Like Pasta to Me!

There are two commonly-used types of variables: string variables and numeric variables. String variables are labels used to identify storage areas reserved for letters, numbers and/or symbols, and are identified with a letter or letters followed by "$" such as N$ or ST$.

Numeric variables are used to create spaces for entry of numbers only. You identify numeric variables by using just a letter or letters (without the "$") such as T, TR, or

STR. The distinction between string variables and numeric variables is necessary because the computer can do math computations *only* on numeric variables.

If this sounds confusing, just try to imagine that one day you decide to organize all the papers in a closet by putting everything in separate boxes. You put all instruction books in one box, garden catalogs in another, repair manuals in another, and so on. You label each box so that you know exactly what is in it.

Then imagine that in the closet you also have a pile of bills and receipts. You put these in separate boxes because you will need to find and calculate the receipts separately at income tax time. You label the boxes with the bills and receipts differently so that they can be identified easily. When you finish organizing the papers in the closet, you have a closet full of boxes, all labeled so that you know exactly what kind of information is in each box; the labels on these boxes do not change, even though you add items to them or remove items from them.

When you assign variables to the computer memory, you are simply making use of the "storage boxes" in the computer: you tell the computer what kind of items you want in each box and how you want it labeled. Then, when you give the command, the computer will go to the correct box and put in exactly what you tell it to; or it will show you what is in the box; or it will add, subtract, or do other calculations with the numbers in the box; or it will print out the information stored in the box. Your house should be so organized.

So much for variables. Once you get used to using them, they'll be as easy to use as paper towels— and a lot neater.

Now back to the program.

40   PRINT "STREET ADDRESS";

50   INPUT SA$

All these commands have been explained, but they should make much more sense now, especially when viewed together. Line 40 instructs the computer to print out the words "STREET ADDRESS," and the semicolon indicates that the cursor is to stay in place right after the last "s" in "ADDRESS."

When the computer reads the next line (50) and comes to the command "INPUT," it will put a question mark after the word "ADDRESS" and then wait for an entry from the keyboard. When the program runs, the printout will look like this:

STREET ADDRESS?

SA$ is the string variable that tells the computer that whatever is entered from the keyboard (for example "34 Clark Street") goes into the space labeled SA$. After the information is entered from the keyboard, the computer will go on to the next lines, which are:

60   PRINT "CITY, STATE, ZIP";

70   INPUT C$

Once again, these commands are a minor variation of the other lines: they tell the computer to print out the words "CITY, STATE, ZIP " Wait for the information to be entered, and then put the information into the space reserved for C$.

The next lines are:

80   PRINT "TYPE: 1 JUNIOR 2 SENIOR
      3 FAMILY";

90   INPUT T

These lines are one other minor variation of the lines above: the computer will print out:

TYPE: 1 JUNIOR 2 SENIOR 3 FAMILY?

But, since the response here is a number (i.e., 1,2, or 3) rather than a combination of letters and numbers, the response will go into a numeric variable in the computer storage space labeled "T."

The next line is:

100   PRINT "THE ENTRY IS"

You probably know what this line means by now. When the program runs, the computer will print:

THE ENTRY IS

The next four lines are all variations of the same command and similar to other print statements:

100   PRINT N$

120   PRINT SA$

130   PRINT C$

140   PRINT T

In line 100 "N$" follows the print command, rather than a word or words in quotation marks. This print command instructs the computer to print whatever is stored in the space labeled "N$." The next line instructs it to print whatever is in SA$, the next line whatever is in C$, and the next line the number that is in T. Each printout will be on a separate line because the commands have been written on separate lines with no controlling punctuation that indicates where the next character will appear).

And, at last—

150   END

This command signals to the computer that the program ends here. In a simple program such as this, it really isn't necessary to put this command in, but it is a good habit to develop.

These are all program lines, or lines you type in or enter into the computer. Some of the explanations include what will happen when the program runs so that you will understand the entry lines better, but you should understand that *entering* and *running* a program are two separate processes. If we go back to the cake analogy, *entering* the program is somewhat like putting all the ingredients together; *running* is like baking the cake.

It may be helpful to review the entry information with very brief explanations (shown in italics) of each line now that we've gone through the whole program. The entries are:

10 REM A SIMPLE PROGRAM IN BASIC;
      ADDRESS FILE   *Remarks line*

20 PRINT "NAME";   *Print instructions*

30 INPUT N$ *Reserve space/ask for name*

40 PRINT "STREET ADDRESS";

                                           Print instructions

50 INPUT SA$ *Reserve space/ask for address*

60 PRINT "CITY, STATE, ZIP"; *Print instructions*

70 INPUT C$ *Reserve space/ask for city/state/zip*

80 PRINT "TYPE 1 JUNIOR 2 SENIOR
          3 FAMILY";   *Print instructions*

90 INPUT T   *Reserve space/ask for type*

100 PRINT "THE ENTRY IS"   *Print instructions*

110 PRINT N$	*Print N$ (name)*
120 PRINT SA$	*Print SA$ (address)*
130 PRINT C$	*print C$ (city/etc.)*
140 PRINT T	*Print T (type)*
150 END	*End of program*

Now that the program has been entered the computer can take over. This is the time when you can sit and watch while the computer does the work, as promised. As soon as you enter the RUN command (this command may also vary with the computer you are using), the program will run.

When this program runs, the computer will stop and wait for a response from the keyboard after each question mark. A fictional name and address have been put in the appropriate spaces as responses and are underlined so that you can identify them and then see what happens with this information.

As the program runs, the printout on the screen or paper will look like this:

NAME? JANE SMITH

ADDRESS? 34 CLARK STREET

CITY, STATE, ZIP? BATH. NY 13579

TYPE: 1 JUNIOR 2 SENIOR 3 FAMILY?

THE ENTRY IS

JANE SMITH

34 CLARK STREET

BATH, NY 13579

2

You will notice that none of the commands, line numbers, or remarks is printed out when the program runs, because the computer only prints out what it is instructed to print out. The term "printout" may be misleading; whether the program prints out or shows on the screen depends on the computer you are using.

This type of program has endless possibilities for use. For example, with modifications, you could have this program print out just the names and addresses, or have this program run over and over again to include more names and other information, or change it in any other way you want to make it more useful to you.

You could add program commands that would allow 100 names and addresses to be entered (or more, depending on the computer you are using). Other commands could have the program run just the names that are identified with either a 1 or a 3 or any combination you want; other commands could print a list of the names only, separate addresses by zip code, state, type, or any other way; and other commands could figure the membership fees, calculate the tax on the fee, list the names of members who have paid and those who have not, or do any other type of listing or calculating for you.

These additional commands require additional knowledge of computer functions and programming, but they are relatively easy commands and could be used in many other programs, so it would be wise to learn what they are and how to use them. And, as in so many other areas of learning, once you understand the basic principles, it is much easier to add to that knowledge and build on the foundation you have.

Remember, when you write a program, all you have to supply is the brain power—the computer does all the work for you. Remember also that the more you learn about the computer, the more you can use your brain power and creativity to make the computer work for you.

CHAPTER 7

MAKING THE PROGRAM MORE USEFUL:

Double the Work and the Computer Still Doesn't Complain

The program outlined in the previous chapter can be used for one task only: to enter and print out one name, address, and category. This program may appear to contain a long list of instructions just to print out a single name and address, but the program does illustrate the amount of instructions a computer needs even to do one simple task, and it does use many beginning program commands that could be used in many types of programs you might write.

It is unlikely that anyone would write a program to do a simple task such as listing only one name and address, but if you add just three more types of commands and make a few changes in the string variables, the same program can be used to keep an entire list of names, addresses, and categories. The new program could have as many names as the memory of the computer you are using allows.

Let's look at the program again, but this time with the added commands, and I'll demonstrate how these changes can easily be put into the program and also introduce some very valuable computer commands at the same time. The lines added to the program will be marked with an asterisk (*) to distinguish them from the lines in the original program. Those line numbers left between commands in the original program are used here for the additional commands.

Although only three new types of commands are added to this program, one of these is repeated in four different statements. These additional command lines make the program appear much longer and more complicated, but are actually just repeat commands added to provide those complete and precise directions the computer must have.

The new program looks like this:

```
 10    REM A SIMPLE PROGRAM,
          ADDRESS FILE
*12    DIM N$(100)
*14    DIM SA$(100)
*16    DIM C$(100)
*17    DIM T(100)
*18    I=0
*19    I=I+1
 20    PRINT "NAME", I;
 30    INPUT N$(I)
*35    IF N$(I)"END" THEN GOTO 150
 40    PRINT "STREET ADDRESS";
 50    INPUT SA$(I)
```

```
60    PRINT "CITY, STATE, ZIP";
70    INPUT C$(I)
80    PRINT "TYPE 1. JUNIOR 2. SENIOR
         3. FAMILY";
90    INPUT T(I)
100   PRINT "THE ENTRY IS"
110   PRINT N$(I)
120   PRINT SA$(I)
130   PRINT C$(I)
140   PRINT T(I)
*145  GOTO 19
150   END
```

Once again, I will explain the changes line by line. In the first change, six lines were inserted between the remarks and the first line of the program. The first four of these are almost identical:

```
12  DIM N$(100)
14  DIM SA$(100)
16  DIM C$(100)
17  DIM T(100)
```

In each of these lines the DIM stands for *"DIMEN-SION"* and indicates the "dimension," (or the size or number) of spaces reserved for the variable that follows the "DIM" (the number is shown in parentheses). In computer talk, this is called "dimensioning the array." Once again we must break away and explain another term, but this is an easy one to learn.

An "array" is just a way to keep variables in order. In the last chapter we talked about having the computer organize information in "storage boxes" that would each be labeled. When you "dimension" the array, you indicate to the computer the number of boxes you want reserved for each label (or variable).

The "DIM N$(100)," indicates to the computer that you want to store information and label it "N$," and the (100) tells it that you want 100 "boxes" reserved for N$. The entries that follow indicate that you want 100 boxes labeled SA$, 100 labeled C$, and 100 reserved for T (remember, the letter without the "$" indicates that only numbers will be put in this space).

Since the computer is such a precise and highly-organized device, it keeps track of those "boxes" by numbering them in order, so it will label the boxes N$(l), N$(2), N$(3), and on to N$(100); it will do the same for SA$, C$, and T. And all this without ever once groaning, "Do I have to do it *again?*"

Now we can return to the program—and now that you know what four of the new lines mean, have an idea of what dimensions and arrays are and how they are used—the rest is easy!

The next change in this program is the addition of lines 18 and 19, which both relate to the same concept, so we'll go over them at the same time. The lines are written this way:

18   I=0

19   I=I+l

The first line indicates to the computer that you want it to reserve a space labeled "I" for a numeric variable. The "=0" indicates that you want that space cleared of any numbers that may have been there from previous programs, and that a zero should be put in the reserved space labeled "I." Many computers will automatically put a zero in any numeric variable space when a program is first run, but this is a good habit to develop in case you have a computer that doesn't.

The next line, "I=I+1" is not an algebraic equation (as it might appear to those who have a math background), but rather a BASIC programming line. This line indicates to the computer that every time it comes to this line, it should add 1 to the number that is currently in the space set aside for "I."

The first time the program runs, the number in "I" will be 1; the second time, the computer will add 1 to 1, and the number will be 2; the next time it will add 1 to 2, and the number will be 3, and so on. This is a method which uses the computer to count or to keep track of the number of times something happens in a program. In this program, the "I=I+1" will be used to keep track of the number of names and addresses entered. The variable used in this way is often referred to as an "index."

Computer programmers commonly use the letters "I" and "J" when assigning a variable name to indicate an index for counting. You can use any letter of the alphabet, but now that you have learned to use terms like "variables," "arrays," "dimensions," and all those other computer terms, you won't want to spoil the image by using something like a "W" here.

The next line changed is line 20, which now looks like this:

> 20   PRINT "NAME",I;

This line instructs the computer to print out the word "NAME" (just as before) when the program runs, but since I have added a comma after "NAME" the computer will leave a space after name and then print the number of the entry (a comma can be used to indicate that you want a space left in the printout). The number printed out will change each time the computer prints the word "NAME," because before it gets to line 20, it will have added 1 to the number in "I" and will then print out what is in "I" now. The question mark will then follow the entry number.

Line 30 is changed only by the addition of the (I) after the string variable. This changes the string variable to a *subscripted variable*. This is another BASIC term you must learn. A subscripted variable means that you have indicated the exact location in the array "N$" where the computer is to put the information you have just entered; this also tells the computer where to look for the information when it is to be retrieved.

Line 35 introduces another new term to your rapidly expanding BASIC vocabulary. It also adds some programming skills you are likely to use often. And it is the last new term used in this book, so you can rest on your laurels after this one.

Line 35 looks like this:

> 35   IF N$(I)="END" THEN GOTO 150

The "IF" indicates that you will give the computer two options when it gets to this line. If you enter someone's name for "N$" the computer is to go to the next line. But, if you enter "end," the computer is to go directly to (written GOTO) line 150, which tells the computer the program is ended.

Lines 50, 70, and 90 are basically the same as line 30, with only the name of the subscripted variable changed.

Lines 110, 120, 130, and 140 are just commands to the computer to print out or show on the monitor what is in each of those subscripted variable "boxes."

Line 145, "GOTO 19," instructs the computer to go back to line 19 rather than to go on to the line with the next highest number. The GOTO statement directs the program sequence back to the beginning of the program, allowing you to enter another name (this command can also be used to direct the computer to jump ahead to another line, as in line 35).

Because this GOTO command directs the program to follow a circular pattern that repeats over and over and over, it creates what can be called a program *loop*. (There are other BASIC commands can also create programming loops) The computer will continue to follow the GOTO command over and over again—day and night if the computer is left on—unless you program a command to allow you to get out of the loop.

In this program, line 35 allows you to enter "END" if you

And finally, the END

want to get out of the loop; that command will direct the computer to go directly to line 150, which will end the program.

The "END" will end the entry part of this program, just as before. When the command "RUN" is entered, the program will run just as the earlier program did, except that this time it will continue asking for name, address, and so on, until you enter 100 names (the limit set by the dimension statement) or until you enter "END".

Thus, the program would look like this when run (of course, any names, addresses, and categories could be substituted for the fictional ones underlined):

NAME 1? JANE SMITH
ADDRESS? 34 CLARK STREET
CITY, STATE, ZIP? BATH. NY 13579
TYPE: 1 JUNIOR 2 SENIOR 3 FAMILY? 2
THE ENTRY IS
JANE SMITH
34 CLARK STREET
BATH, NY 13579
2
NAME 2? JOHN JONES
ADDRESS? 28 STONE STREET
CITY, STATE, ZIP? SUMMIT. PA 35790
TYPE: 1 JUNIOR 2 SENIOR 3 FAMILY? 1
THE ENTRY IS
JOHN JONES
28 STONE STREET
SUMMIT, PA. 35798
1
NAME 3?
and so on........

Now you have a program that is much more useful. And look at how far you have come: in only two chapters you have learned many BASIC programming commands and are well on the way to learning a programming language. And you now realize that nothing in BASIC computer programming is beyond the grasp of anyone.

This program could be used for many purposes if you added other commands, but those just described should give you an idea of some of the information and instructions you need to know for this type of program.

These commands and computer terms can also be used in many other types of programs in many different ways. The use of these commands in other programs is limited only by your imagination and the limits of the computer you are using.

The program above has been very carefully written and checked and should run without any problems. But you should know that occasional problems do occur in computer programs. Since the computer is virtually incapable of making a mistake, when problems occur in a computer program, you almost always have to look for *your* mistake. These mistakes or problems are called *bugs or glitches*.

Glitches are more commonly associated with power surges in the current coming into the computer and are frequently beyond your control. But bugs are another matter, not totally unlike household bugs: you need to get rid of them!

If a program has bugs, you must "debug" it—really! When you debug a program, you must go over it step by step to find any errors. Often the error is nothing more than a missing comma or semicolon, a misspelled command or word, a misplaced symbol, or something similar. But even one of these minor mistakes can cause the program to stall after it starts running, not run at all, or do something you don't want it to do.

When you write programs, it is very important to plan every command carefully. One of the traditional ways to do this is to use a *flowchart*. A flowchart is a way to diagram a program and show every step of the program in sequence. This allows you to visualize the entire program before it is entered into the computer. It is not necessary to use a flowchart to write programs, but this method is very helpful to many people.

Part of learning to write a computer program is learning to check carefully every line and every letter, symbol, or character in the program before it runs, and also learning to debug the program if it doesn't run as planned. But once you have learned to plan ahead and work carefully and accurately, you will be ready to take advantage of the technology of the computer and make it work for *you*. That's a fitting reward for anyone.

CHAPTER 8

THE REST IS UP TO YOU . . .
WHERE DO I GO FROM HERE?

The intent of this book is not to teach you every thing there is to know about computers (no one book could do that anyway), but rather to give you an introduction to computers and to dispel some of the myths about computers, to ease some of the fears surrounding the computer, and to show you how a computer can work for you.

Although this book barely scratches the surface of computer knowledge, I hope it has tempted you enough to make you want to learn more. I also hope the descriptions of the many uses for a computer have shown you how you can put one to work for you.

The information covered here is a good background for learning about what a computer can do, but since each model and brand of computer is somewhat different from every other brand and model, it would be almost impossible to describe all the individual variations in the operation of each of the types of computers. So, the next logical step is to continue your learning at a computer.

Computer instruction is available at every level and from many sources: computer stores, high schools and colleges, community associations, training centers, private instructors, and more. Courses from beginner through college level are available in most areas. Some instruction is available at little or no charge, and other instruction is available at prices ranging from nominal fees to the more expensive college credit courses. Many colleges offer non-credit courses, which are usually less expensive and don't require the course work or exams, making them doubly appealing to many people.

Whatever your needs and circumstances, you should be able to find computer learning somewhere. Hands-on training is important for beginning computer users, and the hands-on is the most important part. While it may be possible to learn a little about using a computer just by watching someone else, if you want to really put a computer to work for you, you need to learn by using a computer. If courses are not available, then instructional videos, learning programs on computer disks, or a good book can be alternatives to an instructor who can watch your progress and answer questions immediately.

No matter what type of instruction you choose, you will need to spend time at the computer and practice using a computer to become familiar with all it can do for you. Whether you plan to use a computer in your home or in a current or prospective career, additional computer instruction will help you to make maximum use of the computer and all its capabilities.

If you plan to use a computer at home, computer learning can show you how to make the best use of programs to help with finances, volunteer work, hobbies and special interests, informational needs, community affairs and any other use that suits your individual needs.

If you are planning to enter the work force, learning to use a computer may be more than helpful: it is probably going to be essential. Computers are used in just about every field of work, and any job that does not include computer use now is likely to include computer use in the very near future. The demand for workers who have some degree of computer proficiency is increasing rapidly, and learning to use a computer will surely help you to find a better job or to advance in a new or existing one.

If you are considering starting your own business, a computer can be an invaluable aid in both the planning and the operation of such a venture. Programs are available for assistance in projecting costs and analyzing information about prospective businesses and for keeping records if you do start a business.

Some educators predict that in the very near future "computer illiterates" will lack the skills necessary to function adequately within society. If you want to understand the type of school work your children are doing or help them with the homework they are likely to have these days, you'll need to know something about computers.

This book was written entirely with the aid of a computer, of course. I used a word processing program to type in the rough draft, then to change words, lines, sentences, and whole paragraphs (many, many times).

Using the word processor saved hours of work and reams of paper. Corrections and revisions were made by pressing the appropriate key rather than by retyping or making corrections in longhand (both methods now seem archaic).

Once the manuscript was written, the cover, pages and graphic illustrations were all created with a page layout program, and then the whole book was sent to the printer on a computer disk. The printer used the computer disk to print out the pages for the book. No typesetting was required to produce a book--just a computer disk. Isn't that amazing?

This book was born out of the frustration I experienced in trying to learn enough about computer use to get through a beginning computer course. The prospect of using a computer and trying to learn anything about how a computer worked terrified me. Assurances that I did not need any math or science background always came from people who had studied both math and science. Books and instruction manuals were of very little help. Stories about the wondrous feats a computer could accomplish only added to the frustrations.

But I persevered. I also had help from a very patient husband, who is well versed in computer learning, to guide me. Not everyone is fortunate enough to have that kind of help available. I know there are many people who have those same fears about computers that I used to have and who need to know they can learn to use a computer, no matter what their background. And so this book.

Few knowledgeable people will deny that computers are here to stay; fewer still will deny that our lives will change because of them. The changes the computer brings will surely be for the better, but only if you are prepared to use them to your advantage. I hope this book has helped you prepare for those changes and has given you the confidence to learn more about using a computer to help with your future.

The information age offers unlimited challenge and opportunity, and computer learning can help you take advantage of those challenges and opportunities. Anyone can learn to use a computer, but I can only provide the inspiration. The rest is up to you . . .

Please let me hear from you and let me know how learning to use a computer has made your life easier, better, more fun, or whatever. I wish you well in your computer learning.

GLOSSARY

ADA: A programming language developed for the Department of Defense as a standard language to be used for its computers. Ada was named after Augusta Ada Byron, Countess of Lovelace, a pioneer in the development of the digital computer (in the 1830's).

ALGOL: ALGOrithmic Language, a programming language used primarily for scientific applications.

ALPHANUMERIC: Any combination of letters, numbers, and/or symbols.

ARRAY: As used in programming, a kind of variable, which can hold a series of values that are related to each other.

ASCII: American Standard Code for Information Exchange. Files saved in this format are plain text files which contain no codes related to the originating software.

BASIC: Beginners All-purpose Symbolic Instruction Code. A high-level programming language, designed for beginners and suitable for many kinds of programs. BASIC is a programming language noted for its ease of use.

BAUD: A term used to describe the speed at which data is transmitted (generally referring to modem transmission). One "baud" means transmission of one bit per second. The term "baud" is derived from the name of Emile Baudot, an early pioneer in electronic communication.

BINARY: As used in computers, Base2 mathematics, which is a numeric system that uses only two numbers: zero and one.

BIOS: Basic Input/Output System. BIOS is a set of program commands contained in ROM and activated when the computer is first turned on. The BIOS performs very low-level initiation of the computer startup and may contain other instructions needed by the computer for its operation.

BIT: Short for BInary digiT. The smallest indivisible unit of computer operation and memory. A bit can have a value of zero or one. A series of bits makes up a binary code. A series of eight bits makes up a byte. From the electronic standpoint, a bit is the presence or absence of power in the electronic circuits represented by a "1" or a "0".

BOOT: To start up or turn on the computer. The initial loading of the disk operating system into the computer memory.

BUFFER: A temporary storage area used to hold data, commonly used in printers, communications programs or other input/output devices. A buffer may physically exist in the input/output device, or as a separate box, or in a separate part of the computer memory. See also *cache*.

BUS: Hardware inside the computer that allows the various parts of the computer to communicate with each other.

BUG: A mistake in a computer program, either in entering code or design (logic) of a program. Bugs may produce problems in the running of a computer program, such as improper output or complete cessation of the run.

BYTE: A group of eight bits. Bytes are the units used to measure the storage capacity of a computer memory and other devices, such as hard or floppy disks and buffers.

CACHE: A temporary storage area on the hard drive, floppy disk or RAM where data is stored for more rapid transfer. Data stored in cache can be transferred faster than from disk. A cache improves the overall performance of the computer.

CARDS: Circuit boards plugged into the computer expansion slots. These cards can add features such as an internal modem or sound board.

CD-ROM: Compact Disc-Read Only Memory. A CD-ROM looks much like a CD music disc, but contains computer software and data. A CD-ROM can hold up to 640 megabytes of data, and is used only for reading data. The usual CD-ROM and drive cannot be used to delete or to save additional data; thus the "Read Only Memory" designation. There are

CDs and drives that can both read and write data, referred to as a Writable CD-ROM; one type is called a WORM (Write Once, Read Many).

CHARACTER: A number, symbol, letter, or space.

CHIP: In computer usage, usually refers to a silicon chip. A silicon chip contains an integrated circuit, and many of these chips are used in the electronic circuitry of a computer.

COBOL: COmmon Business Oriented Language. A programming language designed for business applications.

COMMAND: An instruction to the computer.

CONVENTIONAL (OR BASE) MEMORY : The first part of a computer's memory; the first 640K of memory; the only memory that can be used by DOS without memory management software. See also *extended memory and expanded memory.*

CPU: Central Processing Unit. Usually meaning the main computer chip inside your computer, but may also be loosely applied to the motherboard in computer or to the box which contains the CPU.

DATA: Any type of information (letters, numbers, symbols, graphics) that can be processed or stored in the computer.

DATABASE: A collection of information stored in computer memory or on disc or CD-ROM. Also information accessible by phone lines through a modem.

DEBUG: To find mistakes in computer programs and correct them.

DIGITAL: A system which uses digits as a series of electronic on and off switches (represented by zeros and ones) to represent numbers, letters, and symbols which can be combined to form instructions and data.

DIGITAL COMPUTER: A device which uses a series of binary digits (zeros and ones) to represent information and perform tasks. Microcomputers are digital computers. Other types of computers include analog, fluidic, and optical.

DIRECTORY: A group of computer files grouped together on the hard or a floppy disk. A directory can be used to organize files in logical or convenient groups.

DISK: Same as disc. A circular piece of plastic or metal that is coated with magnetic material. Either of the two types of disks, hard or floppy, are used by a disk drive to record or retrieve information or instructions for use by the computer.

DISK DRIVE: An electromechanical device used to record or retrieve information on a disk. There are two types of disk drives: hard or floppy.

DOS: Disk Operating System: A group of programs that coordinate the operation of the various programs that are on disk or in computer memory; also supervises input/output functions and other tasks necessary for the operation of the computer.

DOT MATRIX PRINTER: A type of printer that forms characters, letters and numbers by placing dots in a grid pattern on the paper.

DTP: Desktop Publishing. Combining text and graphics in a document to produce newsletters, brochures, etc.

DUAL-DENSITY (OR DOUBLE-DENSITY): A method for allowing twice the usual amount of information to be put on a floppy disk.

DUMP: Transferring data from one storage area to another, such as from RAM to buffer.

DX: The versions of the CPU using a complete set of internal commands for processing computer programs and data. Usually used with a chip designation such as 386DX or 486DX. See also SX.

E-MAIL: Electronic Mail. Sending and receiving messages by using a computer, a modem and an E-mail service. Services can be found on CompuServe, America Online, Prodigy, Delphi, and, of course, the Internet.

EGA: Enhanced Graphics Adapter. A lower resolution version of computer display. Usually refers to both the monitor and the supporting hardware in the computer.

EXPANDED MEMORY SYSTEM or EMS: A method of adding memory and supporting software to the computer so that this memory can be used by programs. Sometimes used by certain DOS programs to allow access to more memory.

EXTENDED MEMORY: A method of adding memory to the computer so that this memory can be used by programs. Often used by Windows and Windows programs to allow access to more memory.

EXPANSION SLOTS: Connectors or sockets inside the computer used for plugging in such as sound cards or internal modems. Connector sockets are on the motherboard.

FORMAT: To prepare a disk for accepting files. In a sense creates a road, maps and signs that the disk drive can use in recording and reading data and programs.

FORTRAN: FORmula TRANslator. A high level programming language used primarily for mathematical and engineering applications.

FLOPPY DISK: A computer disk made of flexible (thus the designation "floppy") material, generally enclosed in a stiff plastic jacket. Floppy disks come in several sizes.

FLOWCHART: A step-by-step diagram used to design a computer program.

GIGABYTE: One thousand megabytes. Actually 1,024 megabytes. Abbreviated GB, GIG. That's *lots* of bytes, but terabytes are already on the horizon.

GRAPHICS: Line drawings, special characters, symbols, charts, graphs, or pictures.

GLITCH: Erratic response from the computer, usually caused by power fluctuations.

HARD COPY: A printed copy of anything the computer displays on the screen.

HARD DISK: A disk made of hard plastic or metal coated with a magnetic material. A hard disk has much more storage capacity than a floppy disk and is usually permanently installed as part of the computer.

HARDWARE: The physical components of a computer system, such as the computer, monitor, printer, keyboard, and so forth.

HIGH-LEVEL LANGUAGE: A computer language that uses simple English words for computer commands.

ICON: An image or figure that appears on the computer screen and represents data, commands or programs.

INPUT: Process of putting information or data into the computer.

INPUT DEVICE: A device used to put information or data into the computer. A keyboard, trackball, joystick, mouse, and light pen are all input devices.

INPUT/OUTPUT (IO) DEVICE: A unit that can be used either to enter information into a computer or retrieve information from the computer. A disk drive is an input/output device.

INTERFACE: A device for allowing computers to communicate with each other or with other devices such as a modem or printer. Also used as a verb meaning "to connect." Often overused in conversation.

INTEGRATED CIRCUIT: A small chip of silicon that contains complex electronic circuitry that can be used to run computers as well as many other modern devices.

INTERNET: A huge group of interconnected individual networks containing vast amounts of information on corporations, government, educational institutions, and much, much more. Once for government use only, the Internet is now available to anyone who has the necessary computer equipment and online access.

KILOBYTE: 1,000 bytes. A kilobyte is actually 1,024 bytes, but is referred to as 1,000 for convenience. Abbreviated "K" or "KB" after a number to indicate the size data of storage, such as in "720K floppy disk".

LINE NUMBER: A number at the beginning of a line of a computer program, usually used in BASIC programs. The computer executes the program line by line, beginning with the line with the lowest number and progressing to the next highest.

LOAD: The process of putting a program or information into the computer memory.

LOOP: Continuous repetition of a series of programming instructions.

LOW-LEVEL LANGUAGE: A computer language that uses the binary coding; this programming language is difficult for most humans to understand.

MACHINE LANGUAGE: The only instructions a computer can understand without translation by a high level language.

MAINFRAME: A very large and usually very expensive computer, used primarily by large corporations, government installations, and other groups which must process huge amounts of information.

MEGABYTE (MB, MEG, or Meg): One million bytes (actually 1,048,576 bytes).

MEGAHERTZ OR MHZ : One million Hertz. A unit of frequency used to denote the speed at which commands, data, or programs cycle through the computer.

MEMORY: The part of the computer where programs and information are loaded and/or stored. In the modern microcomputer, memory is generally a solid state device in the form of many integrated circuits (chips).

MICROCOMPUTER: A fully-operational computer, usually based on an integrated circuit microprocessor. Also known as a PC or Personal Computer.

MICROPROCESSOR: An integrated circuit (silicon chip) that contains the Central Processing Unit (CPU), along with supporting circuitry. May contain thousands of transistors, resistors, and so forth, but is generally no bigger than an inch or two square.

MIDI: Musical Instrument Digital Interface. A system of connecting electronic musical instruments to the computer to be controlled by the computer.

MODEM: Short for MOdulating/DEModulating. A device that converts computer signals into a form that can be sent or received over telephone lines.

MONITOR: A unit similar in outward appearance to a television set, but used to display computer output.

MONOCHROME: Using only one color to display computer output.

MOTHERBOARD: The main circuit board in a computer.

MULTIMEDIA: The use of images, sound, text, and graphics (and any other media forms, such as movies, videos, animation, and more) combined for use in a computer program. Multimedia programs are often used for games, entertainment, educational, business and professional use at this time; other uses are being introduced rapidly.

MULTIMEDIA PC or MPC: A standard specification for developing and running CD-ROM software.

MS-DOS: Microsoft Disk Operating System, the operating system licensed by Microsoft Corporation. PC-DOS or IBM-DOS is the operating system licensed by IBM.

MULTI-TASKING: An operating system that allows the computer to perform more than one task at the same time.

NUMERIC DATA: Data made up of numbers only.

OCR: Optical Character Recognition. The process of converting an image or a picture of text into a format that can be used in a word processing program.

ONLINE: Connecting your computer to one of the many services available by using special software, a modem and telephone line to access the information from those services.

PATH or PATHNAME: A sequence of directories and subdirectories that tell where a program or data is located.

PENTIUM: The trademarked name assigned by Intel, a CPU manufacturer, to a fast, high capability computer chip.

PORT: A socket(s) on the computer to which you can connect various devices. Ports may be serial, parallel, game, or other.

RAM: Random Access Memory. The system memory that holds programs and data while being worked on by the computer. RAM is volatile and information in RAM disappears when the computer is turned off.

ROM: Read Only Memory. The permanent memory in the computer. This memory is installed in the computer when it is made and cannot be erased or changed, except by physically installing a new ROM chip.

RS-232: A standard used to denote the rules of connecting a computer to a serial device, such as a modem.

SCANNER: A device that converts photos, images, or text into a digital format that can be read by certain computer programs.

SILICON CHIP: Same as chip.

SOFTWARE: The programs used by a computer.

STATEMENT: An instruction or command in a computer program.

STRING VARIABLE: A variable that can contain alphanumeric data, such as numbers, letters, punctuation marks, or any combination of these.

SVGA: Super Video Graphics Array (or Adapter). A high resolution system of computer display. SVGA usually refers to the monitor and supporting card and software.

SX: A stripped-down version of the full featured (DX) computer chip. Usually used with a chip designation such as 386SX or 486SX.

SYSTEM: All the components of a computer, such as the keyboard, modem, disk drive, printer and software.

TERABYTE: One *trillion* bytes, or one thousand gigabytes.

TERMINAL: A keyboard and monitor combination. A terminal may not necessarily have the capabilities of a complete computer, but is connected to one. A personal computer can be used as a terminal.

VARIABLE: In computer programming, a space in computer memory used to define a storage area that may hold numeric or alphanumeric data. The values for the data can be different at different times.

VESA: Video Electronics Standards Association. A group of companies that determine standards for high resolution computer displays.

VGA: Video Graphics Array (Adapter). A popular medium resolution standard for computer monitors and supporting cards and software.

VIRUS: A program specifically designed to change programs or data in memory or on disks. The effects vary but the general intent is to do harm.

USER FRIENDLY: A computer system or software that is easy to use.

WORD PROCESSOR: Computer application software that allows text to be entered, changed, printed or stored easily. Also, a dedicated device for doing word processing.

Index

Computers Made *Really* Easy for Beginners
by
Norma Leonardi Leone

To order additional copies, fill out the form below and send to:

Lion Press & Video
PO Box 92541
Rochester, NY 14692
Phone: (716) 381-6410   Fax: (716) 381-7439

Quantity discounts are available for classroom use
or for premiums. Write or call for information.

Also available: WordPerfect Instructional Videos (DOS 5.0/5.1)
   Featuring Norma Leonardi Leone
   Introduction I: A Guide to the Basics (35 min.) $29.95
   Introduction II: Continuing with the Basics (70 min.) $39.95
   Easy Macros: Time Savers (30 min.) $24.95
SPECIAL PRICE with any book order:
All 3 videos for only $69.95 (includes FREE Shipping for Videos)
   Write or call for detailed brochure

Computers Made *Really* Easy for Beginners
   _____Copies at $8.95 each   _____
WordPerfect Instructional Videos
   _____ Sets at $69.95 each   _____
Shipping: ($2.00 for one book, $.75 each additional)   _____
(NYS residents only: add 8% tax on total plus shipping) _____

                                   Total _____

NAME: _____

ADDRESS: _____

CITY: _____

STATE: _____ ZIP: _____